MW00779369

"This book is so needed for mothers. Bravo!"
—Lisa R. Gray, mother, speaker, counselor and author of
They Don't Tell, Child Abuse: A Mother's Perspective

"Langston focuses on the experience of the mother who learns her child has been sexually abused. This is enormously significant in understanding the full picture of childhood sexual abuse, and in healing the wounds that it causes. Mothers are often blamed; the mother's subjective experience includes her guilt, blame, confusion, and pain that she has been unaware of her child's abuse. This book is timely and necessary if we are to fully address the wounds of childhood sexual abuse and try to fully heal them for the victims and their families."
—Ellen Nasper, PhD, Assistant Clinical Professor, Department of Psychiatry, Yale School of Medicine, Clinical Conference Chair, Connecticut Society for Psychoanalytic Psychology.

"Given the notion that one's attachment to others is compromised after a traumatic event, an essential goal in my practice is to help restore connections wherever safe and possible. From this frame of reference, acting in a way that positively influences the outcome of trauma is as essential as the individual work necessary in recovering from the traumatic event. Langston's book provides a keen perspective on the dilemmas seen through the mother's experience, as well as offering practical assistance to guide her through this often perilous and grieving terrain."
—Leslie Reed, LCSW, practicing therapist
Long Island and Manhattan, New York

"When a mother finds out her child has been sexually abused, her life is thrown into chaos. She faces devastating choices at a time when she feels as if she is drowning. The pressure is intense: a supportive response on her part will bolster her child's recovery, while a negative response will exacerbate her child's trauma—sometimes for a lifetime. Just when her child needs her the most, she is caught in a whirlwind of emotions and challenging decisions. Until now, she has had to face this gauntlet with little effective support. But thankfully, Langston and colleagues have created an easily accessible, supportive guidebook designed specifically for these mothers. With the publication of *What Do I Do Now?* they have cast an invaluable lifeline into turbulent waters. Every mother of a sexually abused child should buy this book."

—Laura Davis, co-author of international best seller, *The Courage to Heal* and author of *I Thought We'd Never Speak Again*

"For Impact Productions produced Emmy-nominated "The Tale," starring Laura Dern, based on a true story of child sexual abuse. *What Do I Do Now? A Survival Guide for Mothers of Sexually Abused Children (MOSAC)* will be a critically-needed resource to help mothers and families prevent and help their children recover from sexual abuse."

—Simone Pero, Founder, For Impact Productions

This invaluable book is a much-needed resource offering specific supports for mothers and children in coping with the nuclear fallout of this traumatic event."

—Jennifer Fox, Director, Producer of "The Tale"

"Mel Langston has created a comprehensive resource needed for decades, including interventions and answers for mothers of sexually abused children."

—Robert E. Haussmann, PhD, former Dean of Psychology, Northcentral University, Prescott Valley, AZ

What Do I Do Now?

A SURVIVAL GUIDE FOR

Mothers of Sexually Abused Children
(MOSAC)

What Do I Do Now?

A SURVIVAL GUIDE FOR

Mothers of Sexually Abused Children
(MOSAC)

MEL LANGSTON, PhD
with Leona Puma

ISBN: 978-0-578-83127-5 (print)
ISBN: 978-0-578-83128-2 (e-book)

The advice and strategies found within may not be suitable for every situation. Neither the authors nor the publisher shall be liable or responsible for any loss or damage allegedly arising from any information or suggestion in this book. Readers are advised to consult with a professional when appropriate.

Readers should be aware that Internet Websites offered as citations, sources and/or references may have changed or disappeared between the time this was written and when it is read.

The epigraph, a quotation from *Surviving Sexual Abuse* by K. Brown, is used by permission of Lion Hudson pic, Oxford, England.

Cover design by Laura Duffy Design
Interior design by Alan Barnett

DEDICATION

To all mothers and sexually abused children, with our sincere hopes for resilience, recovery and healing.

CONTENTS

Contents

ACKNOWLEDGMENTS

With deepest appreciation to: Jessica Wolf, PhD, committed colleague and editorial collaborator whose motivation, inspiration and drive have been essential in writing and publishing the Guide; Betty Gale Davis, EdD, sister, role model, supporter in all endeavors; Robert Haussmann, PhD, for his invaluable assistance in developing the MOSAC website; Roger Bruce McNellie, PhD, LCSW-S, DCSW, for his thorough reading of the manuscript, advice, counsel and assistance during the project; Attorney Peter Janci, for his recognition of the importance of the Guide, his support of all families struggling with child sexual abuse and his unflagging efforts to obtain justice in child sexual abuse cases; Erin Merryn, President of Erin's Law, for her encouragement and support in writing the Guide; Attorney Mary Ann Murk for essential assistance with legal system content; Laura Davis, co-author with Ellen Bass of the seminal work, *The Courage to Heal*, and author of *I Thought We'd Never Speak Again*, about reconciliation of estranged family members, some as a consequence of child sexual abuse, for her support and encouragement; Joy Robson, a mother in *Leaving Neverland*, for her keen interest and support; Tarana Burke, #MeToo Founder, for her support of our work; Simone Pero of Impact Productions for her intuitive understanding of mothers' struggles, and for including MOSAC in HBO viewers' resources for the documentaries *Leaving Neverland* and *The Weight of Gold*; Jennifer Fox, Director of *The Tale*, based on her personal story of being groomed and sexually abused in the equestrian world, for her strong support; Lisa R. Gray, for her courage in writing her memoir, *They Don't Tell* and her thoughtful review of our book; Susan Kintner, MPH, MSW, PhD, for unflagging support and helpful reviews of the manuscript; Leslie Reed Shields, LCSW, for her insights into the struggles of mothers and their sexually abused children; Ellen Nasper, PhD, psychotherapist and teacher, for her frankness about the work of helping mothers of sexually abused children and her thoughtful manuscript review; Marilyn Johnson, M.A., editor and long-time friend, for editorial advice, consultation and excellent suggestions; Audrey Bernstein, M.S., LMFT, for her wise counsel; Steve Zeoli of Safer Society Press, for his encouragement and beyond-the-call-of-duty assistance in locating out-of-print resources; Mark Sichel, CSW, therapist and author of *Healing Family Rifts,* for guidance about the possible impact of this work on child sexual abuse survivors; Marilyn Allen, literary agent, for encouraging the development of the book proposal, asking key questions, and for her co-authored useful authors' handbook; Nancy Monson, for advice about book publishing; Oprah Winfrey, for her unflagging attention to and support for child sexual abuse survivors, and for presenting the HBO and OWN Special following the *Leaving Neverland* screening; Fernita Wynn, for her collaboration with the authors in organizing Oprah Winfrey's February 2019 HBO Special; Laura Duffy for an evocative book cover design; Maureen Sonntag for careful proofreading; Alan Barnett, for high quality interior design and typography; Michael S. Gross of The Authors Guild for valuable legal advice; each other, for colleagueship and perseverance in the journey of writing and publishing this Guide; our children and families, who mean the world to us.

FOREWORD

Dr. Langston and colleagues have identified an important link in the treatment of child sexual abuse.

Most child protective services professionals view the mother's role in child sexual abuse as a role confusion issue and very often blame mothers for what they knew or should have known, offering her little to no support as mothers face a very complex family issue.

Many mothers are so overwhelmed with guilt as they think back over their possible complicity that it is difficult for them to move forward and provide the support their children need. Formal recognition and acceptance that their child has been sexually abused while in their care is too much to assimilate and can deeply affect their self-esteem.

This book is a great idea and one that I feel is also needed for Child Protective Services (CPS) workers and other staff in the field of child sexual abuse. While I think most professionals recognize that the mother can be the key to the child's healing, the current system does not help the mother much in the process from investigation to court to treatment to follow-up. The mother is often treated as a co-perpetrator and punished, not helped, pushing her to a defensive posture when she is likely already feeling guilty. Often CPS involvement adds to the destruction of the family and the long-term damage of the child.

Providing mothers and families a resource that helps with insight, guidance, and support, increases the likelihood the mother, child and family will be able to begin the healing process.

Professionals will benefit from this book through developing insight into ways that mothers can be helped to better support their children and their families.

Roger Bruce McNellie, PhD, LCSW-S, DCSW
Director, Child Protective Services
Texas Department of Family and Protective Services (retired)
Nacogdoches, Texas

PREFACE

I recall it as if it was yesterday. I was sitting on the edge of my bed, talking to a good friend and mentor about my 12-year-old daughter's recent disclosure of sexual abuse. "Give me a book. Give me something with a list of what to do when this happens to you," I said to my friend. She didn't offer me a book. No one offered me a book. And the only help or support I received would just make the situation worse. I had no answers, I had no prior knowledge, and I had no information available to me at that point. This was 1980, before smartphones and Google and easy access to information, before TV shows, movies, and talk shows about sexual abuse. I had not been sexually abused as a child and knew no one who had. I felt like I was lost in a maze with no way out. And I had believed the promise that it would never happen again.

The first disclosure had come when I was six months pregnant with my sixth child. The principal at school had called, asking me to come to the school, because he had received a report from another parent that my daughter had talked with their child about sexual abuse. I recall leaving work in tears, frantic with fear, and even then, believing it was true. He had asked me on the phone, "Is this possible?" and I had said, "yes." This may sound like a strange answer, since I had no familiarity with sexual abuse. I simply believed my husband was capable of committing unimaginably "wrong" behaviors. Through the years I had discovered so much and had already been so hurt and betrayed. I said "yes" because of the pornography, the times he left home for weeks at a time, living a hidden second life in another state, of his being with prostitutes. Much later, I found out so much more, but at that point, I simply believed that anything might be possible.

The school principal had known my husband for years and confronted him privately in his office before meeting with both of us. I was told by the principal that it would never happen again, that my husband had made this clear to him. It really wasn't my husband talking at all during that meeting. It was the principal, his old pastor, a family friend—not an authority or someone objective enough to know what the ramifications of this light-handed approach would be. The principal offered to help me find a counselor for my daughter. When I didn't hear back from him for two weeks, I called, and he told me he couldn't help me because he had not reported the abuse. It was 1980. Sexual abuse wasn't talked about. And I had no idea what mandatory reporting was. I recall that, after that meeting, I threatened to kill my husband if he touched my daughter again. He promised never to do so. That turned out to be a lie. And it took more than two months for me to discover that. Much later I found out that ultimatums and threats have no effect on an offender's actions.

My daughter's first disclosure occurred in May. In August her little sister was born. I remember thinking, when I held my infant daughter, that her father was a danger to her, too. She was two weeks old when my older daughter came to my room and sat on my bed, saying she wanted to tell me something. I remember the fear coming up. It was true. He had abused her again. On the night her little sister was born, after he had been in the delivery room with me, after he had held his new daughter, he went home and sexually abused her.

I called a good friend, and she and her husband came over that night when I confronted my husband. When my husband initially denied the abuse, this "friend" suggested that perhaps my child was lying – in front of my daughter. What I found out then, what is still true now, is that people do not "want" to believe that sexual abuse occurs, or that it occurs in anyone's life whom they know, or that it could possibly occur in their own families. My husband left home that night, stayed away for three days, came back, confessed it was true, and started counseling.

I was beside myself, with a two-week-old baby daughter and five other children. My daughter had been abused for a period of years without my knowledge. At that time, I did not know how long or how severe the abuse had been. My feelings ran from confusion to hatred, from helplessness and a depth of grief I had never experienced, to a passionate determination to find a way to get through this, to get my daughter help, and to survive.

I believed my child and never doubted she was telling me the truth. I knew I couldn't trust my husband. Sexual abuse was only a vague concept to me at that time, without images or coherent thoughts, but I was aware of the evil, the danger, and was sick with fear. I started having panic attacks, and the stress affected my physical health almost immediately.

I had reached out for help as soon as my daughter disclosed. However, on the night of the first disclosure, a trajectory of "misses" in getting effective help occurred for both my child and myself. Friends either did not believe my daughter, minimized her "story," or consistently and often said I should stay with my husband, he could get counseling and help, and the family shouldn't be disrupted. I was told to forgive him. I was told I couldn't put rules and guidelines for him in our home. The first counselor my daughter saw stopped seeing her because she wouldn't talk to him. Many people knew about the abuse: my daughter's doctor, her counselor, my counselor, my husband's counselor, the attorney who later handled the divorce. But no one reported the abuse.

It wasn't until later, when I realized I had to do whatever it took to protect my children, that I filed for divorce, and he gave up his parental rights in 1982. My husband never received any consequences for what he did. Until the divorce, and often since that time, I was the watch-guard, always on duty, always alert and aware to make sure my children were safe. What I discovered through many years was that sex offenders are very, very smart. And I was unable to protect, even when I thought I was protecting! And children don't tell. Often children in the same home do not know that siblings are also being abused. Sometimes, they do know. It is all heartbreaking and destructive for children. "Damaging" is too light a term to describe the effects of sexual abuse on a child. How do they ever survive the atrocities committed by adults who have a primary responsibility to protect them?

The story after my divorce is a long one that includes moves, therapy, sex offender treatment for my husband, remarriage, further betrayals, another divorce. I found and utilized support for both my children and myself. Together we gathered strength for healing. We moved forward through the maze, the chaos, the damage. My children married, had children, were protective parents themselves, determined their children would never suffer as they had, whether from direct abuse or from the abuse inherent in living in a fractured, incestuous family system. As adults, my children are beautiful, successful. None succumbed to the most destructive outcomes of child sexual abuse.

However, they all continue to struggle with issues related to their childhood. I see this. I know this. The very fact of this motivates me to write this Survival Guide. I continue to live with the fact of my children's sexual abuse. It is a haunting thing, a motivating thing, that causes me to want to prevent other children from being sexually abused, that causes me to want to help other families not to suffer as much as my own. It took years to get where I am now. My relationships with my children will never be what they would have been without our shared family history. Facing reality, not avoiding pain, living in the present, and cherishing relationships is the only path to healing.

It took years of learning about sexual abuse, studying, finding answers, and regretting prior decisions and directions. The early part of this journey was a very hard road, full of pain and grief. Anxiety, hypervigilance, and my alert status was always set to "on." This was my life. I was determined to make a difference, though; determined that other mothers wouldn't have to experience what I experienced. I completed my undergraduate degree in psychology and immediately entered graduate school. I was able to focus on family and addiction, with a specialization in sexual abuse, and my internship was at a sexual abuse-specific mental health agency. I was able to start a non-offending spouse group for mothers, to start a parents' group for parents of adolescent sex offenders, to work with victims, and to work with adolescent and adult sex offenders. This began the rest of my story. I became a therapist, specializing in trauma and family work, as well as addiction.

It wasn't until I was working on my doctorate, though, that I was able to return to a long-held dream, which was writing a book so that other mothers had something to read, a "guidebook" after disclosure. However, now there was internet, and a website made sense. In a special project during my PhD work, I was able to put together the MOSAC website (www.mosac.net), launching it in 2010. Through a survey posted on the website, I gathered statistics for my dissertation about the effects of disclosure on mothers. Those statistics are significant, showing that almost all mothers suffer trauma at the time of their child's disclosure, that the majority of mothers develop symptoms of posttraumatic stress disorder (PTSD), and that most mothers suffer negative health effects due to stress.

I continue to advocate for the protection of children—through work with court systems, through the website, MOSAC Facebook page and mothers' Facebook group, and MOSAC Twitter, providing information about sexual abuse and prevention. In my private practice, I am a trauma therapist, working with victims and mothers. I respond almost daily to the same questions I asked: What do I do next? How do I handle this? Will I survive? My mantra is "Believe your child. Support your child. Protect your child."

The answer to the question, "Will I survive this?" is "Yes, you can survive." I offer my own story as evidence. You will never forget your child was sexually abused. You will carry it with you, in your heart and mind, for the rest of your life. And you will watch your child for the rest of his or her life to see what the consequences of that abuse are in your child's life. You have to live out the answer to those questions.

It was finally time to create a Survival Guide that mothers can hold in their hands, while also using the MOSAC website as a resource. I am excited about reaching more mothers. I hope and pray you will benefit from this Guide, and it will help you in your journey through and beyond the tragedy of having a sexually abused child. There is life for you after disclosure! This Guide is here to help you.

Mel Langston, PhD
Astoria, Oregon

"For me to be able to heal...to recover from my secondary abuse as the non-abusing parent...I do not need to be victimized or rescued; nor do I need to be punished for what happened to my children. Like most non-abusing parents, I have already crucified myself with feelings of guilt for what my children experienced. I do not need to run the gauntlet of suspicion and mistrust, or endure aloofness and indifference."

—Brown, K. (1998), *Surviving Sexual Abuse*

INTRODUCTION

This Survival Guide is designed specifically for mothers who have experienced the sexual abuse of one of their children. Life is difficult for mothers following the disclosure of a child's abuse, and few resources are available to you. Sometimes you don't have supportive family or friends. You may have very little knowledge about child sexual abuse and need to understand what has happened to your children and to you. Most mothers of sexually abused children say that they need and want help following disclosure. This Guide is designed to be a source of practical information about sexual abuse that offers support and resources to help you navigate. It will be complemented by connection with a website with in-depth information for mothers of sexually abused children.

Disclosure is an uninvited, devastating sudden change in your child's life and in yours. Your child is afraid of the consequences of disclosure, and you mirror your child's fear. Your child may experience extreme ambivalence about having made the disclosure; children often recant afterwards, changing or denying their story. Children recant primarily because they fear repercussions as well as their mothers' and others' distress because of the disclosure.

Your child has the same feelings of betrayal and hurt regardless of whether he or she is under or over 18 at disclosure. Disclosure precipitates a long-brewing crisis in which your child of any age is in desperate need of your belief, support and protection. It is a mistake to think your young adult "child" or adult "child" is any less in need of the non-offending parent's belief, support and protection.

The child's first story is the one to believe. Children do not lie about sexual abuse. This is why you must know how to respond when your child talks about his or her sexual abuse. Your response may be the decisive influence in your child's ever again talking about the abuse. An attentive, supportive, calm mother instills a feeling of safety and trust in her child.

While you must be the primary believer and support for your child, you are likely to feel ambivalence about your child's disclosure. Though you believe your child, you may also doubt this could be happening or could ever happen. Your role is to believe and support your child, doing what needs to be done, although you may be filled with confusion and conflicting emotions.

Disclosure of a child's sexual abuse is traumatic for children and mothers. Your responses are affected by your relationship to the perpetrator, your coping skills, extent of belief, life stress, personal life history and anxiety. When the perpetrator is a spouse, family member, or friend, you will struggle with compounded grief and betrayal. Your emotional reactions are similar to those of your child. You experience shock, denial, anger, guilt, confusion, grief, fear, anxiety, and depression. Your child has experienced serious losses, including loss of trust and identity. If the abuse did not occur over a long period of time, and if your child is believed and supported, negative effects may be mitigated. **Your support is the single best predictor of your child's recovery**. Although your child may appear to have no problems related to the abuse, she has internalized severe trauma and needs help understanding her thoughts and feelings in a safe environment with safe people.

Children's trauma response results in repression of thoughts and feelings connected with the abuse, often with observable physical symptoms. Children often feel damaged, resulting in lowered self-esteem, and distorted views of themselves and others. Other common reactions are guilt, fear, depression, lack of self-control, anger, inability to trust, lack of boundaries, sexual acting-out, and pseudo-maturity (acting more mature than your child's chronological age). Victims need to grieve the damage to self, belief and values; loss of innocence, childhood, self, and relationships. Your child's ability to deal with grief and loss affects his or her adult ability to trust, be independent, self-aware, feel positive self-esteem and a sense of control. *Children will often feel complicit with some aspects of the abuse. They often receive special favors from the perpetrator and may believe perpetrator's stories about the "shared secret." These can seriously worsen the damaging effects of the abuse.*

Your child's sexual abuse negatively affects all family and close friends who know about it. You worry about your children and the long-term consequences of the sexual abuse. Your child may have been interviewed for the sexual abuse report and by community agencies, law enforcement, social services, child abuse assessment centers, and the court system. You may initially be in shock and denial. Your reactions will be noted by professionals evaluating your child. Early therapeutic help is beneficial. Your emotional health can either assist or impede assurance of your child's safety and recovery. *The system is not your child's friend; your child is simply not believed by all parts of the system. The presence of a supportive mother or other adult figure is critical to your child's emotional well-being during reporting, investigation and legal action.*

You often have no one around you who understands the hell you are living through; you may have very little support. Sometimes mothers are blamed by others and told that the abuse is their fault. They are given harmful advice and told not to believe the child or not to report. If the perpetrator is your partner or another child, feelings of pain, anger, and confusion increase. Difficult decisions are required. When the perpetrator is your husband, partner, other family member, or friend, you will feel betrayed. Though a devastating discovery, accepting that a stranger has abused your child, is far easier than learning your child was harmed by someone you loved and trusted. Dealing with ongoing consequences of abuse by a family member is very painful. Unfortunately, family members are the vast majority of child sexual abuse perpetrators.

As a mother of a sexually abused child, you are engulfed in a painful, chaotic, and unpredictable crisis. This Guide aims to provide you with specific, practical answers to many frequently asked questions, to guide and assist you in understanding yourself and your child, and to provide options for and direction in effectively navigating the very difficult path on which you find yourself.

What Do I Do Now? takes you through the feelings and practicalities of being a mother of a sexually abused child (MOSAC). **Chapter 1** describes your feelings when you learn of your child's sexual abuse; **Chapter 2** informs you about sexual abuse: what it is, who abusers are, warning signs of abuse, why children usually don't tell, predictable stages, prevalence and effects. **Chapter 3** explains disclosure: immediate effects on your child and yourself, why and how disclosure is unpredictable and erratic, your response, believing your child. **Chapter 4** focuses on legal

3

action. **Chapter 5** addresses support. **Chapter 6** offers skills for parenting your sexually abused child. **Chapter 7** teaches how to protect your child. **Chapter 8** focuses on your recovery and healing. The **Appendix** offers resources for additional help.

Men are the overwhelming majority of sexual abuse perpetrators, also referred to as abusers and sexual offenders. We refer to abusers primarily as "he," while recognizing that women also perpetrate sexual abuse. The guidelines are the same regardless of the gender of the abuser. Believe the child, report the abuse, support and protect your child.

Many mothers contributed to the information in this Guide, whether as clients, colleagues and/or editorial collaborators. For this reason, we decided to use the "editorial 'we'" in the **Guide**. We refer to children as "he," "she," and "they."

We recognize that not all moms will be able or choose to follow all the suggestions and recommendations we offer. Each of us is unique and our circumstances vary. **You** are in charge of your life and your own best decider. We encourage you to connect with your inner compass and your "gut" feelings. Do the best you can in your particular situation. You may choose to read a few chapters of the **Guide** at a time and absorb the information before reading others.

We hope the Guide will help relieve some of your pain, help you navigate through the crisis, reduce the chaos, and provide understanding to make the path ahead seem less frightening and unpredictable. You and your child can and will survive; together you can build a more positive future. There is life after the horror of sexual abuse.

PART I

THE LIFE YOU'VE KNOWN IS OVER

When your child discloses sexual abuse, you go into free fall. Nothing you've known seems certain. You are overwhelmed by a cascade of feelings and the pressing necessity to do something about them. Unlike other books about child sexual abuse, this one helps you by naming and describing your many feelings and then educating you about sexual abuse so you can understand what has happened and what you can do to help your child and yourself.

CHAPTER 1

Help! A Nuclear Bomb Has Exploded in My Family!

You're hurting, and you don't know what to do. You have questions, and you don't know whom to ask. You have thoughts, and you wonder if you may be going crazy. You have feelings, and you have no idea how to manage them. **And you have a child who desperately needs you.**

Overview

We're going to start with the reason you are reading this Survival Guide: how you, the mother, are likely to feel when your child discloses to you - or when you find out he or she has been sexually abused. This disclosure sends you into a severe crisis unlike any you have ever experienced.

Who are you, and what do you feel?

Finding out your child has been sexually abused is an emotional earthquake that shakes you to your core. It sends you into deep crisis, fractures your family, and sends you suddenly into unknown territory.

All at once you experience anger, shock, denial, disbelief, fear and dread.

You may find yourself without support and resources.

If the perpetrator is your spouse or partner, you immediately lose that support as your partner becomes an enemy to be feared; or your partner may try to persuade you to believe him rather than your abused child, adding to your acute distress.

If the perpetrator is an older sibling, you are thrown into an intense double bind of protecting the abused child and finding ways to prevent the older sibling from committing further abuse, while as their mother, also continuing to love, support and protect both children.

As family and friends struggle with this disclosure, they too can be non-supportive.

This can leave you reeling with doubts about who you are or thought you were, how you did not know and you did not protect your child.

You may feel profound feelings of failure as a mother.

Your initial reactions to disclosure

- The emotional impact of finding out that your child has been sexually abused is cataclysmic.
- Shock is likely to be your first reaction.
- You have been thrown into a terrible crisis. Your initial feelings may range from horror to numbness, from rage to powerlessness, from acceptance to deep depression.
- For many, the days following the disclosure include unceasing sobbing, nausea, weakness, and inability to think clearly.
- You may feel physical pain, a weight crushing your chest, a sinking, deadening heaviness. You may struggle to breathe.
- You may feel overwhelming anxiety.
- Some describe this crisis time as "hell."
- Guilt, self-blame, shame, bewilderment and confusion, anger, numbing, and feelings of responsibility are all common.
- You are beginning a process of grief and mourning that will continue for a long time.
- Give yourself time to experience your pain, though you will also probably have to make some important decisions quickly.

Your reactions are affected by

- Your child's age and needs;
- How severe the abuse has been;
- How long the abuse occurred;

- Who the abuser is;
- How you learned about the sexual abuse of your child;
- Your life circumstances and personal history.

Emotions you may feel

It's important to understand your emotions so you can learn from and manage them. We'll describe some in more detail below. In later chapters, we will focus on specific skills, supports and actions you can take to help you manage your feelings and choose your actions as you move through this crisis to resolution and recovery.

Checklist of feelings and physical symptoms. After reading the descriptions, check your feelings and symptoms.

FEELINGS	YES	NO
Ambivalence	☐	☐
Anger	☐	☐
Confusion	☐	☐
Denial	☐	☐
Fear/anxiety	☐	☐
Grief	☐	☐
Guilt and self-blame	☐	☐
Shame	☐	☐
Shock/numbness	☐	☐
Other feelings	☐	☐

Continued on next page

PHYSICAL SYMPTOMS	YES	NO
Accident-prone	☐	☐
Anxiety and panic attacks	☐	☐
Depression	☐	☐
High blood pressure	☐	☐
Indigestion	☐	☐
Rapid heartbeat	☐	☐
Trouble sleeping	☐	☐
Other physical symptoms	☐	☐

Shock is a feeling of numbness, "this can't be happening." Emotions and sensations shut down and you feel distanced from yourself and events. What you've learned is so upsetting that you aren't immediately able to absorb and deal with it.

Denial is a normal short-term response following shocking, painful news. It is a lack of acknowledgment of what has happened. Denial may occur for the first few minutes, hours, days or months, or may be ongoing. It may include:

- The fact of sexual abuse, its seriousness or severity;
- Effects and consequences;
- Abuser's identity;
- Abuser's responsibility;
- Need for help.

You may move between denial and acceptance. Denial can feel safer and less uncomfortable than acceptance of painful reality and resulting losses. Continuing denial can affect your ability to care for and protect your child.

Your psychological health influences your ability to come to terms with this new reality.

Accepting this reality is necessary to provide support and protection to your child.

You must move past shock and denial and gather strength to face and deal with the reality of sexual abuse.

In **Chapters 3, 5 and 6**, we discuss how to help your child with your belief, support and protection even when you are struggling with strong feelings of denial and ambivalence. We suggest ways to get help to move forward even though you feel overwhelmed.

Your child is at serious psychological risk if she does not feel you believe her. Your belief is crucial in supporting your child and the most important predictor of your child's recovery.

Ambivalence is the presence of two different strong emotions at the same time. Sorting out feelings is very difficult when ambivalent. You may feel ambivalent about believing sexual abuse occurred, reporting it, prosecuting the abuser, or leaving your partner-perpetrator.

You may fear losing your partner, a powerful double-bind that deepens ambivalence. You love both the offender and your child and must decide whom to support. If you decide to support your partner, you may lose your child. If you choose to support your child, you will lose your partner. If the offender is another of your children, you will experience a similar double-bind.

This dilemma seldom has an easy solution. When a child's welfare is at risk, the answer to the question of "Whom do I support?" appears obvious. However, you may still feel strong ambivalence. You may hope for successful treatment of the offender and restoration of the family. Family reunification, though, causes serious danger for your child. While treatment providers may say that the offender is now safe, no one can know for sure. You must weigh comparative risks, remembering your primary responsibility is to believe, support and protect your child, difficult as this may be.

Confusion is common. When we try to make sense of something outside our ordinary life experience, our thoughts and feelings conflict. When Alice fell down the rabbit hole in *Alice in Wonderland*, she felt confusion, bewilderment, lack of control, and helplessness. You do not understand how this happened, could have happened, or how you didn't know it was happening.

Anger is a normal human response to shock, pain, and betrayal.

- You are often furious after you learn your child has been sexually abused.
- You may be angry at the perpetrator, the victim, yourself, and/or the many people and systems now involved in your life.
- **Children are usually angry at their mothers for not protecting them and not stopping the abuse.**
- Other family members may also be angry at you, holding you responsible for not protecting your child and blaming you; you may be angry at being judged and blamed.
- Some family members never get past denial and never believe and support the victim.

Guilt and **blame** are also common responses.

- You believe you should have known and blame yourself for not knowing.
- You believe you should have seen signs and feel guilty you did not.
- If you did see signs without accurately interpreting them, you blame yourself for not acting and not protecting your child.
- You may now recognize signs of abuse you had not previously acknowledged as meaningful. This is not unusual. You did not interpret clues through the trauma or sexual abuse lens. Instead, you interpreted based on knowledge of normal childhood development.
- Family members may blame you for embarrassing the family by not keeping the secret, especially if the abuser is a family member.
- Your required reporting of the abuse may result in permanent family fracture when the abuser is a family member.

You are likely to feel increased guilt when:

- Your child is young;
- The abuse went on for a long time;
- Your child had evident abuse symptoms;
- You were sexually abused as a child and believe you should have known;

- The perpetrator is your husband or partner and you feel guilty or blame yourself for having chosen this person as a husband or partner;
- You hold yourself responsible for not knowing, not seeing, and not acting.

Fear is a normal response to threat, and **anxiety** is a normal response to the unknown. You are in the midst of a life-altering crisis with unknown outcome. The disclosure throws much of your life into uncertainty. You may have fears about:

- What will happen to you, your child, your marriage and primary relationships, your other children, extended family members, community relationships, jobs, health, finances;
- The legal process, the court process, interactions with social services;
- The perpetrator;
- Whether you are able to support and help your child;
- Your ability to get through this crisis and survive its emotional consequences;
- Repeat sexual abuse;
- Signs of possible abuse;
- Losing your child—your greatest fear as a mother.

You are *terrified* the court will take protective custody of your abused child, and even possibly your other children. You may feel you would not survive if this were to happen.

In **Chapters 4 and 6**, we will discuss legal issues and how you can protect your child.

Shame is a "painful feeling of humiliation or distress caused by the consciousness of wrong or foolish behavior." You may feel ashamed that this horrible behavior and injury to your child has occurred. You are ashamed to acknowledge it to others. What does it say about you? How can you live with yourself not having known or not having prevented it?

Trauma is a psychological, emotional response to a deeply distressing emotional event or experience, overwhelming your ability to cope, leading to feelings of helplessness and dulled emotions.

Posttraumatic stress disorder is an ongoing mental health condition triggered by a traumatic event. Signs include:

- Reexperiencing in nightmares, flashbacks and intrusive memories;
- Avoiding thoughts, feelings or reminders of trauma;
- Negative effects including strong negative beliefs, negativity about self or others;
- Anxiety and panic attacks;
- Irritability, anger and rage;
- Depression with anger at yourself; deep sadness, feelings of worthlessness;
- Physical symptoms including indigestion, sleeplessness, rapid heartbeat, high blood pressure.

You are struggling with many conflicting and painful emotions. You blame yourself for the abuse. You feel desperate, lonely, isolated, ashamed, and stigmatized. You are also afraid of the consequences to your job, profession, and finances. If you lose your partner's financial support, you worry about paying for housing and utilities. Perhaps you were not working outside the home, and now you must find a job. These concerns add to the weight of your responsibility and fear.

Taking care of yourself and having adequate, positive support is essential to your and your child's mental, emotional, and physical health: you are his or her primary support.

You need support as you come to terms with the abuse, help your child/children and move through the aftermath. Chapter 5 focuses on support for you both; **Chapter 6** emphasizes parenting; and **Chapter 7** is about protection.

Most mothers do not know about the abuse prior to disclosure, and most mothers believe their children's reports of abuse. Most mothers, after learning about the abuse, report it, protect their children from further abuse, and advocate for their children.

"Research has consistently shown that false allegations of child sexual abuse by children are rare."[1] **Believe your child, support your child, protect your child of any age, including adulthood.**

Mothers are not all-knowing. You are human. It's important to view your current situation realistically.

Always remember: The perpetrator is responsible for the abuse. The victim is *not* responsible. The mother is *not* responsible. The perpetrator is 100% responsible for his or her actions. He made a choice. He is to blame for the resulting harm and consequences. The victim is *not* to blame for not telling; and you, the mother, are *not* to blame for not knowing.

It is your responsibility to protect your child, despite the impact on your relationship with the abuser.

Chapter 2 includes statistics demonstrating the **frequent occurrence** of child sexual abuse. Together with highly sexualized ads, movies, literature, customs and social media and easily available online pornography, child sexual abuse is much more common than many people realize.

You are not alone. Child sexual abuse is more common than people think, as Chapter 2 shows.

What do you need now?

The **Survival Guide** addresses information and knowledge about child sexual abuse that most mothers need:

- Abuse: what, when, where, how often;
- Your child's reaction;
- What to do after disclosure;
- Sexual abuse signs and symptoms;
- How both child victim and siblings are likely to react;
- Reporting and the legal process;
- Child Protective Services and protective custody orders;
- Options regarding parent custody, no-contact orders, restraining orders;
- Support in making immediate, medium-term and long-term decisions such as whether to separate or divorce, to move, to tell family members and friends;
- How to change the home environment, protecting your child victim and siblings from further abuse;
- Help with grief;
- Acknowledgement by professionals working with the family;

- Space away from family member-perpetrator;
- Feeling respected;
- Regaining control.

In **Chapter 2**, we'll focus on sexual abuse.

CHAPTER SUMMARY

In this first chapter, we've seen that your child's disclosure of sexual abuse results in a severe crisis for you with many conflicting feelings, including shock, denial, ambivalence, anger, blame, fear, confusion, guilt, shame, grief and depression/sadness as well as physical reactions to trauma. You are especially affected by learning that your husband/partner/child's father figure, or an older sibling, is the perpetrator. Your child is also in crisis, having taken the terrifying and courageous step of talking about behavior that is destroying his or her childhood and wrecking your family. Your child has suffered trauma and needs help from you and others to feel believed, supported and protected.

We've emphasized the necessity, in the midst of these overwhelming and conflicting feelings, that you believe, support and protect your child who has been violated by someone previously trusted, has had the courage to tell you about it, and who desperately needs your belief, support and protection.

The author and editorial collaborators are mothers and mental health professionals who have experienced the shock of our child's sexual abuse disclosure and have learned from our own and others' mistakes along the way. All who have contributed to this **Guide** want to help you gain as much knowledge and support as possible so both you and your suffering child can recover from this deep emotional trauma. A healthy, supported mother is in a far better position to aid her child than a desperate, confused and torn-apart mother. Your success in helping your child recover will also aid in your recovery.

CHAPTER 2

Sexual Abuse? I Have No Clue!

Overview

In **Chapter 1**, we identified and explored your feelings after learning your child has been sexually abused.

In this **Chapter 2**, you'll learn:

• What sexual abuse is;
• Who does it;
• How often sexual abuse happens;
• Sexual abuse warning signs;
• Stages of sexual abuse;
• How sexual abuse affects your child;
• What to do if you suspect sexual abuse;
• Recovery from sexual abuse is possible;
• Chapter Summary.

What is sexual abuse?

Child sexual abuse occurs when an offender (abuser, perpetrator) abuses a child victim. The offender may be an adult or an older child. The perpetrator has more power than a child and can force your child into sexual activity. Child sexual abuse is seldom a one-time event and often happens regularly. Most victims know their abusers, either family members (the largest percentage), trusted friends or community members. Sexual abuse by a stranger is much less common.

Sexual abuse is defined as the use of a child to sexually stimulate or satisfy the sexual urges of the abuser. Some examples of sexual abuse are:

- Asking a child to engage in sexual activity;
- Exposing genitals to a child;
- Caressing a child in a sexualized way (stroking, breathing heavily, holding tightly);
- Showing a child pornography or sexually explicit material, including online pictures of genitals or sexual acts;
- Touching the genitals, buttocks, or breasts of a child or adolescent;
- Having a child fondle the perpetrator's genitals;
- Masturbating in front of a child;
- Oral-genital contact;
- Digital penetration;
- Vaginal or anal intercourse;
- Penetrating the vagina or anus of a child with an object;
- Forcing a child to perform sexual acts with another child or with another adult;
- Use of a child in production of pornography;
- Prostituting a child;
- Adults having sex in front of a child.
- Age-inappropriate discussions about sex, including suggestive language and innuendo;
- Allowing or encouraging children to view age-inappropriate sexual media.

Who does it?

Most child sexual abusers are men, although women also sexually abuse children. The National Center for Victims of Crime reports women are perpetrators in about 14% of cases involving boys and 6% involving girls.[2] Most child sexual abuse in families is perpetrated by a husband or partner.[3] Older siblings are also an increasing concern. Known community members commit a significant proportion of sexual abuse. Neighbors, family friends, babysitters, school teachers, coaches, grocery store clerks, lawyers, pastors and other trusted community members abuse children sexually. No group, age, gender, race, religion or ethnicity is exempt. Sexual abusers are young, old, male, female, rich, poor, educated, and uneducated.

How often does child sexual abuse happen?

As RAINN.org points out, "Sexual violence is notoriously difficult to measure."[4] Some reputable sources include RAINN.org, National Crime Victimization Survey (NCVS), Justice Department studies and data from the Department of Health and Human Services and other government and academic research studies.

At least one of every four girls and one of every six boys under the age of 18 is sexually abused before the age of eighteen.[5] Child Protective Services (CPS) agencies report a claim of child sexual abuse is substantiated every eleven minutes.[6] Most child sexual abuse cases are not reported, and, if reported, are not proven because of lack of evidence.[7] Children do not disclose sexual abuse, mainly because most sexual abuse is committed by a family member[8] and most frequently, a parent.[9]

Some reliable statistics:

- Approximately 60 million sexual abuse survivors live in the U.S. today.[10]
- Boys are almost as likely as girls to be sexually abused.[11]
- Children are most vulnerable to sexual abuse between the ages of 7 and 13.[12]
- 20-30% of children have been, are being, or will be sexually abused prior to adulthood.[13]
- 28% of youth ages 14 to 17 have been sexually abused.[14]
- Over 63,000 cases of child sexual abuse were reported **and** substantiated by child protective services agencies in 2016.[15]
- Since only an estimated 30% of cases are reported to authorities, the real number could be more than 200,000 cases yearly.
- 58% of convicted sex offenders reported their victims as 12 or younger.[16]
- In 90% of cases involving rape of an under 12-year-old child, the child knew the perpetrator.[17]

Sexual abuse warning signs: how can you see that it is happening?

Warning signs can alert you to possible sexual abuse or confirm your suspicion. Child victims react to sexual abuse in various ways; no single sign proves that it occurred.

Warning signs may be divided into emotional, behavioral and physical categories. Not all sexually abused children will show signs in all categories.

Emotional warning signs: Presence of a number of the following warning signs suggest that your child may have suffered abuse and is unable to ask for help.

- Anxiety;
- Conflicts with family;
- Depressed mood;
- Difficulty trusting others;
- Extreme mood swings;
- Fear of adults;
- Fear of being alone;
- Fear of certain people or situations;
- Feelings of hopelessness, resulting in thoughts of suicide;
- Guilt and shame;
- Intense anger, hostility, or explosive rage;
- Noticeable loss of self-esteem;
- Phobias, such as fear of doctors, dentists, or sleeping with someone;
- Self-hatred;
- Shyness and timidity;
- Unexplained panic;
- Unexplained sadness and crying.

Behavioral warning signs: Certain child behaviors strongly suggest sexual abuse has occurred because non-abused children generally do not behave this way. Signs include:

- Asking an adult or others to participate in sexual activity;
- Excessive masturbation;
- French kissing;
- Imitating sexualized movements;
- Making sexual sounds;
- Masturbating with an object;
- Penetrating vagina or anus with an object;

- Placing mouth on sexual anatomy of others or themselves;
- Playing with dolls in sexually imitative ways;
- Verbal, physical, sexual abuse of other children;
- Victimizing other children.

Additional behaviors suggesting that sexual abuse may have occurred include:

- Addictions, such as alcohol, drugs, food, or compulsive masturbation and pornography;
- Aggression towards other children or angry acting-out towards adults;
- Changes in eating habits, such as loss of appetite or overeating and eating disorders;
- Changes in school performance;
- Compulsive behaviors, such as repeatedly showering or washing hands;
- Decline in social activities, not wanting to play with friends;
- Delayed social and emotional development;
- Early marriage;
- Hallucinating;
- Inability to focus and concentrate;
- Inability to receive affection, pushing away hugs;
- Loss of interest in activities and hobbies;
- Nightmares or night terrors;
- Promiscuity;
- Running away;
- Self-mutilation, such as cutting;
- Use of adult sexual language.

Physical warning signs often provide **proof** that sexual abuse has occurred and enable doctors to confirm sexual abuse. **If you see any of the following signs, immediately call your child's physician or go to the emergency room.** These include:

- Bleeding, cuts, or bruising in the genital or anal area;
- Genital infections and venereal disease;

- Genital itching;
- Genital odors;
- Pain during urination or bowel movement;
- Problems walking or sitting;
- Redness or rash in the genital or anal area;
- Torn or bloody underclothes;
- Vaginal or penile discharge.

Additional physical signs may show a child's concern about his or her body after the body has suffered sexual abuse. These are not definitive signs. **If they are present with behavioral and emotional indicators, it is cause for strong suspicion**. These physical signs include:

- Fear, dizziness, or nausea when your child sees, hears, smells, or touches something associated with the abuse;
- Inability to control urinary and bowel function;
- Numbness in body;
- Pregnancy;
- Unexplained symptoms such as stomachaches, headaches, frequent sore throats, frequent complaints of nausea, backache, pain in legs and joints, or physical weakness.

What are the stages of child sexual abuse?

Child sexual abuse often follows a predictable pattern. If you know this pattern, you can better understand why children don't tell. A perpetrator *chooses* to abuse child victims. He usually plans how best to approach and gain your child's cooperation, grooming your child so your child is afraid to tell anyone about the abuse and will keep it secret.

Abusers may also groom, manipulate and seduce adults, including mothers and parents. Abusers seek power over others and entrap their victims.

We have also seen egregious examples of institutional complicity and collusion with sexual abuse of children by religious institutions, sports promoters and coaches, famous people and those who serve them. Films such as "The Tale," "Leaving Neverland," "At the Heart of Gold," and "Spotlight" demonstrate multiple situations in which adults allowed sexual abuse to continue rather than face the consequences. Rachel Denhollander's 2018 Victim Statement provides a strong attack on "looking the other way," with her question, "What is a little girl worth?" answered by, "Everything."[18] We will address prevention further in **Chapter 7**.

The usually identified stages of sexual abuse are:

Grooming: the sex offender carefully plans how to approach your child to gain trust so sexual abuse may occur later. Grooming may include:

- Special attention;
- Gifts or money;
- Taking your child on outings;
- Hugging, kissing, and physical contact;
- Invading your child's privacy, such as walking into the bathroom when your child is using the toilet or bathing;
- Lying next to your child in bed or sleeping in the same bed;
- Allowing your child to get away with inappropriate behaviors;
- Talking to your child about topics normally discussed with an adult;
- Talking with your child about sexual activities.

The perpetrator convinces your child that sexual activities are acceptable. Grooming aims to make your child feel safe and willing to be alone with the perpetrator.

Sexual activity with your child:

- The perpetrator now has access to his chosen victim and has gained his or her trust.
- He then engages your child in progressive sexual activity.
- For example: the perpetrator shows your child pornography, later exposes himself, masturbates in front of your child, touches your child's genitals, has him touch the offender's genitals, has oral sex with your child, and attempts vaginal or anal intercourse.
- This sequence may or may not be gradual, depending on the extent of threat and violence.
- Your child is now trapped and is the helpless victim of an adult single-mindedly pursuing his own satisfaction.
- The perpetrator may be convinced he loves your child and is doing nothing that will harm your child.

Keeping the secret: Sex offenders are highly skilled in getting their victims to keep the secret of sexual abuse. They may tell your child:

- "No one will believe you if you tell."
- "Your family will be broken up if you tell."
- Something bad will happen to the abuser, such as having to leave the house or going to jail.
- "You'll be taken away from your family."
- "I'll hurt your mother."
- "I'll hurt your pet."
- "You're bad. That's why you did this."
- "All daddies do this with their children, and it's normal."

Most children *never* tell about their abuse. (See "Why Children Don't Tell" in **Chapter 3**.)

- Disclosure depends on your child's understanding of possible consequences, and the amount of threat and fear.
- The offender has convinced your child that never telling is the only option and will threaten your child with destructive consequences for telling.
- A violent offender will intensify your child's fear by threatening more destructive consequences for telling.
- Children usually will not tell unless pain and confusion are overwhelming.
- Where symptoms of sexual abuse are clear and adults intervene, your child may or may not tell.
- Your child is afraid of what will happen if he tells.
- If the sexual abuse is ongoing, your child may block large chunks of her childhood memory.
- Some tell *years later*.

Disclosing the abuse

Disclosure occurs when your child reveals the secret. **Chapter 3** focuses on many barriers to disclosure, ways disclosure occurs and what may happen afterwards, including suppressing disclosure and repressing memories of sexual abuse.

It is very important that you and other caregivers know sexual abuse signs and act when you see them. You and other caregivers should know perpetrators' typical approaches and behaviors so you can protect your child when you suspect danger.

Adverse Childhood Experiences (ACE)

The Adverse Childhood Experiences (ACE) Study was initially undertaken at Kaiser Permanente Health Plan (KP) in California in 1995–1997 and subsequently became a partnership between KP and the U.S. Centers for Disease Control.[19] Study results showed a direct correlation between ten key adverse childhood experiences, including childhood sexual abuse, and medical and psychological problems in adulthood. ACE Study research is ongoing, and outcomes are consistent with original findings regarding high prevalence of sexual abuse.

The research found that traumatized children suffer more illnesses throughout their lives and have a shorter life expectancy than others. Even more than the immediate harm of abuse, the stress and fear associated with the trauma produce long-term medical risks. Stress worsens many diseases and causes inflammation associated with many health risks. Abuse and trauma lead to eating and sleep disorders, causing more medical problems. Child abuse is linked to depression and PTSD, leading to substance abuse, crime, prostitution, teen pregnancy, school dropouts, self-mutilation, and suicide. Health problems and poor decisions interact with each other to increase risks significantly.

How does sexual abuse affect my child?

Most child sexual abuse victims feel damaged. Negative impacts are likely to be stronger when the perpetrator is a family member.

Child sexual abuse affects your child's emotional, behavioral, physical, social, and spiritual development. The severity of short and long-term impact is influenced by:

- Your child's age when abuse occurred;
- How often the abuse occurred and over what period of time;
- Severity of abuse, including extent of violence;
- Relationship between victim and abuser;

- Your child's support system;
- Extent of protection from further abuse;
- Your child's resilience and coping skills.

The immediate effects of child abuse are related to the stress of the abusive acts and the fear and anxiety they cause. Your child is afraid the abuse will happen again. She feels guilt, shame, and confusion. If the abuser lives in your home, fear and anxiety are daily and chronic.

Immediate effects of sexual abuse are:

- Emotional problems;
- Behavioral problems;
- Somatic (bodily) symptoms;
- Lowered self-esteem;
- Sexualization (age-inappropriate sexual behaviors often seen in sexually abused children).

Responses of boys and girls are more similar than different. The effects of abuse are mediated by your response and the presence of other positive, caring adults in your child's life (**See Chapters 3, 5 and 6**). Your child must be protected from additional abuse. Your support is key in your child's recovery. Dr. Bruce Perry, a leading child psychiatrist specializing in trauma, reports that relationships are the primary mediating factor on long-term effects of child sexual abuse.[20]

Ten effects of sexual abuse on your child:

1. **Damaged goods syndrome**: Your sexually abused child feels damaged, worthless, and unworthy of love. This can result in years, if not a lifetime, of self-sabotage and self-harm. The profound negative effects of the perpetrator's abuse and statements will be lessened by family and friends' support.
2. **Guilt**: Your child may experience guilt about keeping secrets and the sexual behaviors. She may feel responsible. The perpetrator may have blamed your child for the abuse. Abusers lie and manipulate the victim in order to keep the secret. Often warning signs of abuse are misinterpreted as problem behaviors, and your child may feel guilty about these. If she is angry and acts out, she may feel guilty about her anger.

3. **Fear:** Your child is afraid the abuse will continue; she also fears the consequences of telling. He is living in a painful, stress-filled situation, including nightmares, night terrors, and anxiety. His fears of people, situations, sensations, and emotions and conflict are related to the abuse. He may develop phobias, experience anxiety and panic attacks, become suspicious of others, or may approach people and situations fearlessly where fear would ordinarily be warranted. She may fear all men, or approach all men. She may dislike being touched, or may inappropriately touch others. Extreme responses suggest difficulty in self-regulation. Fear is biochemical, not just a "feeling." Cortisol, a stress hormone released when fearful, causes cascading bodily effects. With repeated fear, neurochemical processes adapt, and the brain is hardwired to over-respond.

4. **Depression:** Your child's depression may be a warning sign as well as a result of sexual abuse. Symptoms include sadness, crying, irritability, difficulty sleeping, loss of appetite or overeating, withdrawing and isolating, no interest in previously enjoyed activities or friends, poor school grades, dropping out of recreational or social events, self-harm, and suicidal talk. Your child may seem very tired or complain of illness symptoms doctors cannot confirm - more signs of "crying out."

5. **Low self-esteem:** Healthy self-esteem includes self-confidence and capable and competent feelings. Sexual abuse negatively affects your child's attitudes, motivation, emotional regulation and enjoyment of positive relationships. Your child may have low self-esteem; she may lack friends, be non- assertive, use negative self-talk, and have negative body image along with anger, self-hatred, self-harm behaviors and low self-worth.

6. **Lack of self-control:** Many sexually abused children cannot regulate themselves emotionally and behaviorally and have impulse control problems. Acting-out behaviors may include:
   - Disrespecting adult authorities;
   - Anger; hitting and yelling at peers and adults;
   - Sexually abusing a younger child;

- Stealing;
- Setting fires;
- Hurting pets;
- Adolescent prostitution;
- Running away.

7. **Anger**: Your child may repress anger, seem passive and compliant, a "good kid," without behavioral problems. Underlying anger, hostility and hate may be inside. Victims may be angry at the perpetrator for abuse, and angry at non-protective parents, usually you, for not keeping him/her safe. He may be angry at himself for inability to stop abuse, for deserving to be abused, or being out of control. Repressed anger may turn into depression and withdrawal.

8. **Inability to trust**: The closer the relationship to the abuser, the greater the impact on your child's trust. Primary caregiver abuse results in the greatest harm because your child knows this person is responsible for his or her well-being. This is the ultimate betrayal. Abuse by an older sibling is a significant betrayal, because a sibling would be expected to be protective. Trust is also damaged after abuse by those who are less emotionally close. Trust is also affected by your child's age, how often and how long abuse occurred, pleasure or pain your child experienced, your belief and support following disclosure, and your child's resilience, coping skills, and self-esteem.

9. **Blurred boundaries:** When normal boundaries between parents and children are crossed, an adult has violated a child's privacy and personal space. Sexual abuse violates physical, sexual, emotional, mental, and spiritual boundaries, leaving the victim without personal boundaries and gravely compromised in setting and maintaining personal boundaries in the future.

10. **Pseudo-maturity**: Childhood phases require specific developmental tasks of trust, autonomy, initiative, industry, and identity accomplished sequentially to avoid negative effects later. Sexual abuse interferes with your child's ongoing development,

resulting in mistrust, shame, doubt, guilt, inferiority, and role confusion. Undesirable neuroanatomical and neurochemical changes take place.

Your sexually abused child has experienced serious losses that will affect adult life, including abandonment, lost childhood and relationships, loss of innocence, damaged world-view, sense of self, belief and values, and loss of self. Helping your child to grieve these losses will help restore your child's ability to trust, be independent, self-aware, have positive self-esteem and a sense of control over her life as an adult. Grieving *with* your child may also help you.

You also need to grieve. Because you must focus first on your child's needs, it may be necessary to delay or limit your full grieving while you attend to your child. Your awareness, as well as making time and space for your grieving, are important for your well-being. Counter any feelings of guilt and shame, and actively try to overcome feelings of isolation.

Tasks of grieving for both children and adults include:
- Overcoming denial and accepting losses;
- Feeling emotional pain and working through and beyond it;
- Adapting to current life, role, sense of self, and the world.

Several stages of grief overlap with consequences of abuse. We include them below as they are important to understand.
- **Shock and emotional numbness**: These normal coping responses buffer the initial trauma, allowing adaptation. If pain, fear, or threats were involved, your child does not understand these and may continue to be paralyzed by fear and anxiety, repressing her memory of the abuse.
- **Denial**: With intense loss or trauma, denial protectively shields us. We may deny all or part of a traumatic event. While our minds may accept reality, our emotions may come out in nightmares and other trauma symptoms.

- **Anger and rage:** These are normal, healthy grief responses. People often ask, "why me?" about loss, and are angry at others, self, and God. Your child may not know what happened to her was wrong. The offender may have normalized the abuse or have given apparently rational explanations. Your child is confused and lost. She may direct anger at other children or adults rather than the perpetrator.
- **Guilt:** Also a normal response to grief. Self-blame for the abuse, sadness, shame, and an unrealistic sense of responsibility are common responses to child sexual abuse.
- **Anxiety:** Results from loss of control and freedom, and feeling helpless. Chronic anxiety can cause negative physical reactions, illness and emotional problems including panic attacks, phobias, and negative and obsessive thought patterns.
- **Depression:** Your child may be sad, tired, uninterested in daily life, have sleep problems, and cry often. Grieving and depression are similar. Be watchful; your child may behave self-destructively to soothe herself through eating disorders, cutting, or substance abuse. Depression can result in hopelessness, hostility, self-anger, loneliness, despair, and suicidal thoughts. Professional help is crucial for your sexually abused child and is *urgent* when your child is depressed.
- **Acceptance:** Your child reaches some resolution that abuse was not her fault and is no longer happening; she is safe now, and can go on more positively with her life.

Negative effects may last many years or be lifelong. Because sexual abuse is so invasive and impactful, your child may struggle with negative emotions, addictive behaviors, self-destructive tendencies, physical and mental illnesses, unhealthy relationships, posttraumatic stress disorder, dissociation, sexual disorders, altered brain development, education and employment difficulties, lost potential, hopes, and dreams.

You can provide comfort and support. Safety, structure, and routine assist your child in moving through the stages of grief. Your presence and availability will assure him or her that he or she is not alone. We discuss support more thoroughly in **Chapter 5**.

What to do if you suspect your child has been sexually abused

If you notice one or several warning signs, depending on their severity:

- Call the local abuse hotline in your community anonymously and ask questions before initiating a formal report.
- Call Law Enforcement and the local social services/DHS/Child Protective Services agency in your community or to report the abuse.
- Take your child to the Emergency Room if necessary.
- Call your child's physician for an immediate appointment.
- Call a counselor to discuss your observations.

Guidelines for action

- The more severe the warning signs, the more likely that abuse has occurred.
- Non-disclosure by your child does not mean abuse did not occur. Most children do not tell.
- If you observe a cluster of warning signs, your child is obviously experiencing severe distress, and abuse has most likely occurred.
- When your child's behavior suddenly changes without explanation, sexual abuse is a possibility.
- When your child focuses on bodily complaints and physical symptoms that do not respond to medical treatment, sexual abuse is a possible explanation.
- Be aware that medical and mental health professionals may not be knowledgeable about or sensitive to the possibility of sexual abuse.

Recovery from sexual abuse

While the descriptions above are fearsome and daunting, your child and you can recover from this devastating experience. Human beings are remarkably resilient, even after suffering horrible psychological and physical injury. When safety and support are available, recovery is possible. Recovery takes time and patience, together with belief, support and protection. A supportive and nurturing family, community and lifestyle can be very helpful. We discuss these in detail in **Chapters 5, 6, and 7.**

CHAPTER SUMMARY

We have covered many topics in this chapter to help you understand sexual abuse, who does it, how to find out whether it has happened to your child, how it affects your child, and what to do if you suspect sexual abuse.

Chapter 3 explains disclosure more thoroughly. We also suggest how to show your belief and specific supportive and protective actions to take following disclosure. **Chapter 4** addresses legal issues and interactions with child welfare agencies. We discuss support, parenting, protection, resilience and recovery more thoroughly in **Chapters 5, 6, 7 and 8**.

CHAPTER 3

How Could This Happen?
I've Always Protected My Child.

The Truth about Disclosure and How to Help
Your Child Feel Safe about Disclosing

Overview

Full disclosure soon after abuse is the exception. Many sexually abused children never disclose; many disclose only in adulthood; others disclose small and unclear clues over time. Be alert for the possibility that sexual abuse has happened to your child and create a feeling of safety so your child can disclose painful, frightening information.

This chapter helps you understand that disclosure is complex and usually happens over time, not all at once. We explain how you can help your child feel safe in disclosing to you and what you must do after disclosure to demonstrate your commitment from now on—no matter what—to believe, support and protect your child. We offer a list of actions you can take to show you believe your child and reassure him or her. We help you understand why children don't tell; why you didn't know; immediate emotional and physical effects of disclosure on your child, the family and you; what happens when adult children disclose, and similarities and differences in disclosure and your choices when your child discloses in adolescence or adulthood. We discuss disclosure of sexual abuse by a husband/partner/father figure or an older sibling.

What is disclosure?

Disclosure occurs when a child reveals the secret of sexual abuse. He or she may tell a friend, a sibling, or a "safe" adult. Most children do not tell; only about 38% of sexually abused children disclose or talk about sexual abuse.[21] They may not know whom or how to tell. They do not have the language to tell. They are afraid and do not know whether they will be believed if they do tell.

The term "disclosure" implies that *all* is told. However, abuse disclosure usually occurs in phases. Children must first deal emotionally with the reactions of the person they are telling. They are also afraid of telling the secret because of guilt, shame, threats by the abuser, or fear of hurting another person, usually you.

When children disclose sexual abuse, they watch closely and observe the reaction of the person they are telling. They will remember this moment for the rest of their lives. You also will remember this moment and your response for the rest of your life. This is why your support is so important. Your child must feel believed. Your child will observe your response and judge whether to continue telling or to change their story. Your belief and continued support are essential, as your child is likely to be required to tell other adults what happened.

Remember: If and when your child discloses, it is a remarkable event. He or she is showing extraordinary courage and trust in talking about being sexually abused.

It may be months or years before you learn the full extent of the abuse, or as much as your child (or offender) discloses. You may never know the full extent. Your ability to absorb information about the abuse is affected by your initial shock and your emotional state. You may not initially be able to truly hear and understand what you are told. While shock and denial are normal at first, you must get past these as soon as possible so you can support and protect your child. If you regret that you did not respond with sufficient strength at first, it is not too late to apologize to your child, let them know you were in shock, and that you **do** believe and **will** support them.

How does disclosure occur?

Your child may come directly to you and talk about sexual abuse, or she may have told a friend, a teacher, or another adult. Or perhaps you observed and were concerned about signs of abuse and asked your child. Sometimes children provide verbal or behavioral clues to mothers, and if there is no direct response, they believe these have been noticed and deliberately ignored. Children often believe they have told you, that you already know about the abuse. Sometimes disclosure is accidental, and your child did not consciously intend to tell the secret. Sometimes a child tells a little at a time, giving hints of something wrong, or maybe a few words in an unrelated conversation. Your child may also tell the secret as if someone else were being sexually abused. Children frequently do not have the cognitive skills for the difficult task of disclosing that an adult or an older child, especially a parent or family member, is abusing them.

Your child may not recognize sexual abuse until another child explains it or a friend hears or suspects what is happening. Many children assume the behavior is normal until outside influences convince them it is not, adding to your child's confusion. Life after disclosure often is so different from before that your child feels guilt about having contributed to the change.

Disclosure is encouraged by:

- Someone pushing your child to talk;
- Offender's confession;
- Accidental disclosure to family member or professional;
- Disclosure to another child who reports to parent or teacher;
- Intervention leading to disclosure;
- Availability of a child advocate;
- Your child's maturity.

Disclosure may be suppressed and abuse denied by:

- Someone pushing your child not to talk;
- Loyalty to the perpetrator, especially a family member;
- Threats from and fear of the offender;
- Offender's denial;
- Duration of abuse;

- Dissociation (disconnection from reality);
- Your child's immaturity.

General information about disclosure

Disclosure is related to:

- How long the abuse has been occurring;
- Perpetrator's identity;
- Severity and force;
- Perpetrator's statements, including bad outcomes if your child told about the abuse;
- Your relationship with your abused child;
- Your child's belief that you will believe him or her.

Maternal belief is essential to your child's recovery from sexual abuse—knowing you believed him when he told.[22] If your child does not feel believed, she may stop talking or recant, take back, her description of abuse, saying it was not true. All allegations and reports then cease, all legal actions stop, your child has no protection; and the abuse continues. Most often, your child will never try to tell again, because no one believed him or her. And the perpetrator is free to continue to abuse your child or other children.

Remember: **The most critical time to support and act to protect your child is Immediately after disclosure.** You must encourage your child to express feelings, including fear of the consequences of reporting, while you take action to protect him.

Disclosure also has an immediate effect on siblings, who are secondary victims. When the abuser is a father, brother, grandfather, siblings do not know how to manage their feelings or whom to believe. Anger, confusion, and guilt result. Disclosure may affect many aspects of siblings' lives, including changes in home, school, friends, loss of family structure, stability, trust, and safety. Siblings too need understanding and support.

Somehow you have to manage it all! When the perpetrator is a family member or close family friend or neighbor, it is highly likely that he also abused other children. Siblings should always be questioned. Often one child does not know another child is also being abused; or one child thought she was the only one enduring the abuse and did not know about the child who is now disclosing.

Remember: Most children do not tell about sexual abuse.

Regardless of a sibling's disclosure, another child who has also been abused may be unable to disclose their own abuse. Loyalty to the perpetrator and fear of consequences are huge barriers to telling about sexual abuse. Siblings in blended families may experience divided loyalties. Some siblings may pressure your child to deny what has happened because of family stress resulting from the investigation after abuse is reported.

Medical examination of siblings may be necessary. Advocate for **all** your children. Provide opportunity for siblings to disclose, so they can also receive support and protection. Even if not sexually abused, siblings may be anxious about what people are saying about their family and may react with problem behaviors. Your understanding and support of all your children is essential to help them manage their emotions following disclosure.

What influences children not to tell?

Understanding the many reasons children don't tell can alleviate much of your struggle, guilt and doubt about why you didn't know about the abuse.

Reasons include:

- Love, loyalty and the abuser's role in your child's life;
- Telling a "secret;"
- Not having skills and language or knowing whom to tell;
- Self-blame and shame;
- Fear of:
  - ▸ Consequences to self and family;
  - ▸ Abuser's threats.
  - ▸ Not being believed;
  - ▸ Being blamed;
  - ▸ Destroying the family.

More reasons children do not tell:

- Posttraumatic symptoms, including dissociation (disconnection from reality to lessen emotional pain), depression, and anxiety;
- Young children disclose less often; disclosures increase with age;
- Desire to protect perpetrator from punishment;

- Perpetrator normalizes the abuse;
- Perpetrator's threats and your child's desire to protect self and family;
- Confusion about responsibility for abuse;
- Perceptions about abuser's protection;
- The more severe the abuse, the greater your child's dissociation and the greater her distance from reality;
- Dependence on adults for basic survival needs;
- Developmental needs;
- Belief that parents and adults in authority are to be obeyed;
- Inability to speak about sex due to family/adult inhibition or prohibition against talking openly about sex;
- Previous partial disclosure did not result in belief and protection;
- Belief that mother or parents do not really care about him or her;
- Reluctance to give up perpetrator's bribes and rewards and/or physical affection.

What is delayed disclosure?

If sexual abuse has been ongoing for a long time, your child is afraid adults will not believe him when he discloses. Unfortunately, this is often true. He will be asked why he waited so long to tell. You may have suspected, but not known. You may look back at signs and clues and feel guilty about *not seeing* it prior to your child's disclosure. You may have had limited knowledge of sexual abuse.

If you have a history of sexual abuse, you may fear that you are overreacting to a non-abuse-related sign. Without clear disclosure from your child, your suspicions will result in internal conflict, and you may be unwilling to ask, even indirectly.

Adults unfamiliar with the dynamics of sexual abuse, perpetrator behaviors, and *normal* responses of child victims often do not understand delayed disclosure. No child can explain *why* they did not tell sooner. When an adolescent discloses during a family conflict, or when in trouble, such as following use of alcohol or drugs or running away, adults will usually interpret the disclosure as a way to get out of trouble. When parents have separated or are divorcing, your child may feel safe enough to come forward about his father as the abuser. Courts may mistakenly interpret this disclosure as your manipulation to gain custody. While adults may also interpret inconsistencies as lies, these are far more likely to be developmental communication deficiencies compounded by fear of telling.

Children very rarely lie about sexual abuse.[23] Most children never tell, even into adulthood. Children are more likely to deny, minimize, and forget the abuse. When children's reports of abuse are compared to an admitting offender's report, the child's version is usually understated and appears less serious than it actually was.

Remember: Almost all non-physical warning signs of sexual abuse have an alternative explanation.

Why do children recant and change their initial report?

- Your child
  - ▸ Doesn't feel believed;
  - ▸ Feels guilty and feels responsible for the abuse;
  - ▸ Sees all her fears coming true of what would happen if she told; her account is doubted; the perpetrator denies abuse happened;
  - ▸ Becomes aware the disclosure will cause changes, such as a family member leaving the house or going to jail, and does not want to feel responsible.
- The family may be afraid of public attention or feel shame that abuse happened;
- The offender may put tremendous pressure not to go forward legally;
- Other family members may doubt the abuse and pressure adults not to report.

After the initial disclosure and your report to authorities, your child must disclose to social workers, police, special investigators and interviewers, possibly including doctors and counselors. Everyone now knows what happened to her. It's not surprising she now tells all these people it's not true and did not happen. She wants her life back! If her father is the perpetrator, she and perhaps her siblings may have been removed from their home. *Her family has fallen apart.* Her siblings may be angry at her.

Her family may have to move. She feels she has betrayed her family, feels responsible and may retract or recant the report of sexual abuse, hoping to make everything okay again. And perpetrators and family members may pressure her to recant. It is easier for your child to return to a *pretend okay* family, so she retracts her *story* and restores her family. You and investigators must **not** then be convinced abuse did not occur.

Disclosure is a process, not a one-time event. Any abuse disclosure is incredibly difficult for children, who already feel afraid, confused, and ashamed. They are asked embarrassing questions about what happened. Many children recant or take back sexual abuse allegations after their first disclosure, primarily because they were not believed. Recanting also occurs more frequently when an abused child is younger and a parent is the abuser. However, **most children who recant are telling the truth when they initially disclose.** Recanting is not a result of the child making up a story (a false allegation). It is primarily a result of family influences. Your support of your child through disclosure, investigation and court case is essential.

What can you do if you *suspect* your child has been sexually abused?

Suppose your child has *not* disclosed, although you have seen behaviors or emotional signs that cause you to wonder whether abuse happened? Perhaps you have a gut feeling about a person in your child's life, or you have seen something unusual. While you may notice something wrong, it may take years to learn the truth.

You are faced with the dilemma of interpreting behavioral signals as sexual abuse when an easier explanation makes more sense. This is about the "lens" with which we see. Viewing nightmares, bedwetting or chewing fingernails from a *normal* lens does not suggest sexual abuse. If your child has not disclosed sexual abuse, and if several emotional or behavioral signs are present, and *especially* if physical signs are present, you *must* quickly arrange a professional opinion (pediatrician, emergency room, or a report of suspected abuse). If your husband or partner lives with you, you must ask difficult questions. No matter the response, you **must** obtain a professional opinion.

Circumstances may affect your awareness:

- Domestic violence, the struggle to cope with and protect yourself and children from a physically assaultive partner;
- Marital conflict or disruption;
- Lack of confidence in parenting;
- Health problems;
- Sex offender's manipulation to get what he wants without anyone knowing.

Abusers lie to victims, telling them the abuse is normal, their mothers know about it and it's okay; or, if they tell, no one will believe them; or terrible things will happen to the abuser or child and family if they tell. Fear silences your child and she keeps the *secret*.

Children **almost never** lie about being sexually abused, and abusers **almost always** lie about abusing.[24]

Remember: Children cannot describe activities about which they know nothing or create details about events to which they were never supposed to be exposed.

When the perpetrator is a sibling, another of your children, or other extended family member

The emotional challenge becomes even more complex when the perpetrator is another of your children. You are responsible to support, protect, and act in both children's best interests. You must use wisdom, good judgment, compassion, emotional self-control, and self-support. Your child or adolescent perpetrator cannot leave your home and live independently. Although he may have to leave for treatment, you continue to be responsible for both children. The child-perpetrator is in distress and possibly at significant risk of self-harm or self-destructive behavior. Your loyalty and emotional energy will be split. Your decision to report the abuse is complicated by your fears for your child perpetrator. **Reporting is the only way to obtain help for the perpetrator and safety for the victim**. Your self-blame and guilt are intensified when sibling abuse occurs, as you feel responsible for the perpetrator and may feel a failure as a parent. Your pain, confusion, and ambivalence are increased.

When sibling abuse is involved, additional questions include:
- Was the sibling offender sexually abused?
- How, where, and from whom did he learn this behavior?
- What caused your child to act in this way?
- Has he been exposed to pornography?

Abuse by other familial figures also results in complex and painful situations. Whether the abuser is your father, brother, nephew, best friend's son, you **must report** and protect your child, *no matter what other family members say*!

When your child discloses as an adult

Considering the low percentage of children who disclose, disclosure of childhood abuse by adults is understandable. The disclosure is as emotionally distressing to you as the mother of an adult as it is to mothers of young children.

Your response to an adult child's disclosure must be the same as for a young child. You believe. You do not argue or defend yourself or a previous partner. You listen and focus on your child, not your own thoughts. Though your adult child may now have adult cognitive abilities, his emotions about the abuse are those he had when the abuse occurred. His emotions and experience of your reaction to his disclosure are more similar to those he would have had if he had disclosed in childhood than they are to adult emotional reactions. This is not easy to understand. You must view your adult child's reactions through the lens of a mother of a young child who is also a full-grown adult.

While you may not have to worry about your adult child's current safety with the perpetrator if your adult child and the perpetrator are not living in the same household, and you may not need to report to the legal and social services systems, your belief and support of your adult child will be essential.

The fall-out from adult disclosure can be very disturbing, as adult children disclose egregious acts against them, without your knowledge, by husbands, fathers, partners, grandfathers, whom you love and with whom you've had and may still have long-term relationships. If you learn about your child's abuse years later, you may feel more guilt, shame and self-anger, and the victim may be angrier and more blaming towards you. Expect this, and keep supporting your adult child. Get therapy for yourself. Be aware you may need to make major unanticipated life changes with significant emotional and financial impact.

How do you encourage your young child to disclose?
- Talk with your child in a safe and comfortable place;
- Do not ask her if she is being abused;
- Ask if she is worried, bothered about something, or feels unsafe in some way;
- Keep your questions open-ended;
- Allow your child to offer the information; do not scold or criticize your child in any way;
- Do not lead your child in giving information, suggest what may have happened, or ask for details (to avoid later accusation of coaching).

Ways to support a child during disclosure

You may have been unable to confirm suspicions of sexual abuse or your child may have already disclosed. In both instances, talk with your child. What you hear can elicit a range of emotions. Your task is to give your child a sense of safety and stability. Remain calm. Your ability to be present, listen, and believe your child is critical to him now and in the future.

Remember: Your belief in your child's abuse disclosure is the most important predictor of your child's recovery from sexual abuse.

The following guidelines help you through this crisis and will continue to be useful as disclosure continues over time.

1. **Provide a quiet, safe place to talk**: If your child begins to talk in public, move to a quiet place as quickly as possible. Protect your child by having as few people as possible know about the disclosure. Your goal is to help your child stay safe.
2. **Stay calm**: Your calm attitude will reduce your child's anxiety. Manage your emotions internally. Your child may disclose just a little of the abuse and watch for your reaction. If you appear shocked, angry, disgusted, or seriously upset, she may shut down

and say nothing more. She may also recant or take back what she has already said to protect you from being hurt. The abuser may have used your anticipated reaction and your pain to convince your child to keep the secret. Your child also feels guilt, shame, confusion, and fear. Your response will either reassure your child or increase his negative emotions.

3. **Listen and stay present *with* your child**: Focus your eyes on your child. Do not let your own thoughts and questions interfere with your child's telling about the abuse. As difficult as it can be, do not interrupt and ask questions. Do not press for details. Leave details to those investigating the case. Make sure that your child answers: Who did it? What happened (**not** details)? Where and when? You can share this "bare bones" information with law enforcement. The "who" is essential to protect your child from the abuser.

4. **Keep your *focus* and *attention* on your child's safety and best interests**: Make no comments of doubt, judgment, or suspicion. Do *not* express concerns about what the disclosure means to you, the family, or anyone else.

5. **Say "I believe you:"** Right now, your child must know you believe him. When your child discloses, he is afraid he will not be believed or the consequences of telling will be severe. The abuser has lied to prevent the secret from being told. Let your child know how proud you are of her courage in talking about the abuse, you understand how difficult this is for her, and she was right to disclose.

6. **Reach out and comfort your child:** Provide emotional and physical support. Keep your focus and thoughts right now entirely on your child's feelings and responses. Let your child know that what happened to her was wrong, and she is not guilty, and you want to protect her. Make sure to say, "It's not your fault," and the abuser is 100% responsible. Be very aware of the range of emotions your child may be feeling. Though you are having incredibly painful feelings while listening, stay present and focused on your child.

7. **Take the disclosure seriously**: Affirm your child for disclosing. Let him know abuse happens to other children, many children don't tell, and affirm his courage for telling. Recognize that children frequently give minimal information and report having few memories.

8. **Let your child know you must report what he is telling you so the authorities can help keep him safe**: Otherwise, he may feel betrayed when he finds out that you reported. *Remember*: He has probably been told this is a secret; he has now told the secret and is afraid of the consequences.

9. **Don't make promises**: Although you may want to promise the abuse will stop and will never happen again, you may not be able to keep that promise. You may not have the power to get the abuser out of your child's life. If your child is sexually abused again, he or she will be angry at you and feel betrayed. When the abuser is your child's father, you may not be able to get him out of your home. Without legal charges, you may not have a legal right to remove the abuser from your child's life. However, you and your child may have other options such as leaving and arranging supervised parental visitation. Assure your child you will *always* do your absolute best to keep her safe.

10. **Tell your child you will get help for her**: Explain a counselor is a "safe" person she can talk with about her feelings who will help her feel better. Explain the counselor will be part of a "team" who will help keep her safe.

When your child discloses sexual abuse, your initial talk with her will significantly affect future investigations.

Prepare yourself for these discussions. Make sure you are aware of your feelings. Children are very sensitive to any disconnect between words and feelings or departure from honesty. Be honest.

Remember: Your child must be heard and supported.

Your belief is most important to your child. Otherwise, she is likely to recant or change her story. **You must report**, regardless of your relationship with the offender. Otherwise, sexual abuse will continue; with other children, if not with your child. Remember to include siblings in family conversations, help them feel loved and supported, and also question them regarding their experiences with the perpetrator. **You also need a support system to assist you in negotiating this crisis and its aftermath.**

Actions to take immediately after your minor child discloses:

1. **Immediately report the abuse to your local law enforcement and/or child protective agency.** Do not delay. **Reporting is protecting your child.** Your immediate report will support your motivation and intentions to protect your child. If you do not report the abuse, you may not be able to keep your child safe. You may be questioned regarding your reluctance, especially if the abuser is a family member. *Remember:* Your job is to believe, support, and protect your child. Child protective services will assess you, your family, and your home after the report. When the abuser is your husband, partner, son, brother, supporting your child and reporting the abuser are intensely painful. Put aside your doubt and confusion for now, and do the *right* thing for your child. Be an ***advocate*** for your child.

2. **Also insist on a wellness exam in a Child Abuse Assessment Center or by a Sexual Assault Response Team medical professional.** Referrals are often made by law enforcement and child protective agencies when investigating and bringing sexual abuse charges.

3. **Alert your child's pediatrician and staff that sexual abuse and sexual abuse disclosure have occurred.**

4. **Keep your child safe.** Make sure the perpetrator has **no** access to your child! If the accused perpetrator and your child are in the same location, immediately remove your child from the premises. *No matter who he is,* do not let your child be unsupervised with this person. This may require a Restraining or No Contact Order from your local court, pending completion of the investigation. Your job is to protect!

5. **Do not conduct your own investigation regarding the disclosure.** Investigators will do so, and will talk with the abuser. Try to remain as patient and calm as possible; do not interfere in legal proceedings.

6. **Keep daily functioning normal as much as you can**. Continue a predictable routine with your child. Spend time together, play, and relax.

7. **Arrange counseling immediately**. Find a counselor educated, trained, and experienced in child trauma, specifically child sexual abuse. Your child is vulnerable and needs additional support from a qualified counselor who can be their "voice" in the court proceedings.

8. **Arrange trustworthy professional help for yourself** with an experienced counselor who understands the challenges of mothering while traumatized and in shock.

9. **Protect your child by informing as few people as possible about the disclosure.** You aim to help your child stay safe and calm.

10. **Take care of yourself to prepare for the stressful experiences ahead.** Use coping and stress reduction skills and pay attention to your health. Taking care of yourself helps you support your child. Don't depend on others to look out for your child's best interests. Do all you can to protect your child and yourself during and after the investigation.

What you need after your child discloses:

- Support from close friends, family, and social service and legal systems;
- Information about sexual abuse consequences for your child, yourself, and other family members;
- Information about perpetrators, grooming, why children hold the secret, and disclosure;
- Specific knowledge about the abuse your child experienced: what, when, where, how often;
- Safety from the perpetrator for your child and yourself;
- Awareness of potential family member responses;
- Knowledge about legal reporting and law enforcement, child protective agencies, and court systems, including protection options;

- Knowledge of available support resources, including counseling and medical support for yourself;
- To be respected and acknowledged by professionals working with the family;
- Information about coping strategies;
- Assistance in problem-solving and decision-making.

Challenges for mothers after disclosure

Painful and confusing events usually occur after your child discloses sexual abuse. You will struggle with shock, pain, fear, anger, confusion, guilt, worry and grief. You will wonder how you didn't know. You may have suspected something was wrong; finding out enables you to move forward to protect your child. You may want to deny that this could possibly have happened to your child.

Some professionals will *assume* you must have known about abuse that occurred in your home. Extended family members and even friends may blame you, causing you feel *responsible* for the abuse. As they investigate, social service agencies will observe your emotional functioning. These observations affect their assessment and influence recommendations regarding family intervention and protection.

Remember: The perpetrator is 100% responsible for the sexual abuse. No explanation shifts the blame to you or your child victim. The perpetrator is responsible for the abuse **unless** you are knowingly involved, are not reporting, and are not stopping the abuse and removing your child. Then you are complicit.

Sexual abuse disclosure is extremely difficult for all mothers. Most mothers know the possible short- and long-term effects, and fear the consequences of reporting for their children. When the abuser is not a family member, mothers rarely hesitate to report. When the abuser is a family member—especially your husband, your child's father and/or your partner, whether in a traditional or blended family—your denial is stronger, hesitation more probable, and support more necessary. You are likely to go through self-questioning, revisiting and blaming. It's essential to connect with your pain while also recognizing you are not all-knowing and may in fact have been unaware of what was happening to your child. Working through this betrayal, rage, grief and self-doubt takes time and understanding. A knowledgeable and trustworthy counselor can be of great assistance.

You may respond to disclosure with defenses that can hurt both your and your child's best interests. Defenses may protect you from feeling the full pain of disclosure. Denial is the first stage of grief, and it takes time to accept loss. To demonstrate belief, support, and protection, you must very quickly face the reality of your child's abuse. Your management of the disclosure crisis will affect your child's recovery and family functioning. Victims and siblings require your continued mothering.

It will be difficult to absorb the information and accept the reality. You will experience some of the strongest emotions in your life, while at the same time you are required, for your child's well-being, to be the most emotionally well-regulated you possibly can be.

You must manage your emotions so you don't shut down the "telling" by "overreacting" or "underreacting." Overreaction would be excess emotional response, such as overtly showing shock, hurt, fear, anger, panic. Though you may feel these, remaining outwardly calm gives your child a safe space to talk. Underreaction would be a too cool, non-emotional response, without empathy and compassion. Both can result in continued abuse, because without full disclosure and reporting, your child will not be protected.

Your child must come first. During the "finding out" phase, you must learn everything you can so you can fully understand your child's experience and can effectively support and protect her. Although your child's abuse is traumatic for you, you must maintain a calm presence, giving your child a sense of safety and stability. Your ability to be present, listen, and believe your child is critical to him now and in the future.

Remember: Your child may believe you already knew and you let these things happen to them. They may have been told by the abuser you were aware of it and it was okay with you. Your child may be angry at you because they believe you didn't stop them from being hurt.

Not only must you have the strength and courage to believe and support your child, you must also move forward with the necessary legal actions to protect your child. You may feel torn apart by your relationship with your partner, while your essential commitment is to protect your child whatever her age.

The perpetrator's double betrayal in your relationship and betrayal of your child is doubly painful. Your inevitable resulting ambivalence can impact your support of your child. It is possible, however, to hold the ambivalence inside, and not express it except with a completely trustworthy counselor. While you feel and must overcome your ambivalence, your primary responsibility is to your child.

The abuser's denial is predictable. Abusers know their admission may result in serious consequences. They may vehemently deny, undermine, or minimize your child's account and accuse your child of other negative behaviors. When the perpetrator is your husband or partner, you must struggle not to believe him.

You must cope with many painful feelings while also managing added external demands, including an increase in appointments and interviews related to the report, legal proceedings, and yours and your children's medical care and counseling.

To review: you have discovered your child has been sexually abused, and you are responsible for providing care and protection. You may be so angry and *stressed* that it's difficult to think clearly, make decisions, and give the love and support your children need. If you fall apart, your child blames herself and believes she should not have told. She believes she is responsible for *all* the consequences following disclosure, including her mother's emotions.

Take care of yourself following disclosure

Some mothers may use unhealthy coping to avoid reality, such as drinking, drug use, or overeating. They may reject help; rationalize or minimize the situation; try to escape through TV, movies, gaming; or dissociate, keeping distressing thoughts, feelings, and experiences out of conscious awareness. These offer *temporary relief* from painful feelings and situations. For your child's sake, though, reality must be faced *immediately*.

For some mothers, your child's abuse disclosure may bring back, possibly for the first time, your own memories of abuse. If you have been abused earlier in your life, it is essential to seek therapy for yourself, as your reactions about your own history can be confused with those about your child's abuse. Obtaining help in sorting through these painful feelings is important for both you and your child.

Mothers often experience increased health-related problems because stress can impact health. You may have more illnesses, such as colds and viruses; headaches; nausea and gastrointestinal problems; fatigue; and increased hospital visits and surgeries. You may have difficulty sleeping, impacting overall health and decision-making. However, you must stay healthy for your child. Self-care and healthy coping are essential!

To *cope* is to deal with a problem successfully, to adapt effectively to unanticipated change. Healthy coping skills enable you to face reality, manage distress, and adapt well to difficult circumstances. You may cope more effectively on some days than on others. Don't judge yourself or give up; ask for support. Grief is not static. Pain and energy ebb and flow.

Healthy coping will enable you to survive the disclosure crisis, support your children, grieve and recover. Unhealthy coping will worsen the crisis and may lead to harm to your child, you, and other family members.

Healthy coping skills include self-care activities, such as eating properly, exercising, getting enough sleep, spending time with friends, and taking time-outs for yourself. You need to be clear-headed, rational, and healthy. A solid support system, adequate information and resources, and physical and mental health are essential. **Chapter 5** provides additional information about healthy coping skills.

Recovery following disclosure of your child's sexual abuse requires telling yourself the truth. This means rigorous honesty, including assigning responsibility for the abuse, examining your feelings of guilt, and reality-testing your thoughts. The *truth* includes:

- What's going on right now in your life;
- What happened in the past;
- What may happen in the future.

Do not deny the reality of the pain. Do not pretend everything will be okay. Telling the truth **does not** mean telling **everyone** the truth. This is your crisis, often a private, alone experience. You must choose whom you can trust: protect yourself with self-care and boundary-setting. Unless you choose to confide in a counselor, close friend, or family member, it is not necessary to tell others any of the truths you are telling yourself. These truths involve *what is*, not what you want to be or hope was happening, but *what is*. Telling the truth means facing the good, the bad, and the ugly.

And keep in mind the saying, "The perfect is the enemy of the good." In other words, **do the best you can.** The world is not ideal, and we are not perfect. The well-known Serenity Prayer, can also be helpful: "Higher power, grant me the serenity to accept the things I cannot change, the courage to change the things I can, and the wisdom to know the difference."

Recognize your child will experience effects and consequences of the abuse for a very long time. However, **when** your child is believed, supported and protected, many long-term consequences may be limited or avoided.

CHAPTER SUMMARY

This chapter explored the many aspects of disclosure, its effects on and consequences for your child and you. **Chapter 4** will guide you through reporting and the legal process. **Chapter 5** addresses support; **Chapter 6** is about parenting your child who has been sexually abused; **Chapter 7** discusses protection, and **Chapter 8** focuses on recovery and healing.

PART II

WHAT'S NEXT? THE FIRST THING YOU NEED TO DO; THE LAST THING YOU WANT TO DO

Child sexual abuse is often not reported to the authorities because of fear of violence, denial, distrust of and ignorance about the legal system. We introduce you to the legal system and how it can protect your child.

Criminal cases present both legal and emotional challenges. The legal system is often difficult for a lay person to understand and navigate, aggravating and adding to stressors you, your child and family are already experiencing.

CHAPTER 4

Reporting and the Legal System

Overview

In **Chapter 4**, we help you understand, live through, and successfully manage the reporting and possible criminal case resulting from the sexual abuse of your child. We also describe civil and dependency cases and offer suggestions and tips to help guide you.

Report of Abuse

A child often first discloses to a mandatory reporter including doctors, nurses, therapists, teachers, child welfare workers, and attorneys. Your child may disclose to a counselor, friend, or you. **If your minor child discloses to you, while not mandatory, it is your responsibility to report immediately to law enforcement.**

You may first learn of the abuse from law enforcement or child welfare after they receive a mandatory report and initiate an investigation. A report to law enforcement will usually result in a cross report to the appropriate child welfare agency and vice versa. Once a report is made, focus on obtaining services for and supporting your child. Leave the investigation to the professionals.

- Law enforcement is responsible to investigate, and they often have specially trained sexual assault detectives. To assure a case is opened and will be investigated, begin by contacting law enforcement and follow up with a call to the DHS (Department of Human Services/Child Welfare) Hotline.
- You can call City Police, County Sheriff's Department or State Police.

- Law enforcement will collaborate with the Department of Human Services/Child Protective Services (the names may vary by state).
- The District Attorney's Office may be informed by law enforcement at the time of the report.
- You can report to Abuse Hot Lines; every state has websites with information and numbers to call.
- Individuals who report in good faith are immune from litigation.
- Child welfare and law enforcement are also responsible to assure the child victim is safe.
- Your child should be referred to a Child Abuse Assessment Center and have only one examination and forensic interview (see below).
- Informing your family physician very soon after your child has disclosed sexual abuse and recording the date will help you document your case, though the physician may not be allowed to testify in court.

Although parents are not mandatory reporters, not reporting may be viewed by both law enforcement and child welfare agencies as failure to protect. Be sure to inform your child you have made the report so your child will not be surprised when a stranger appears to ask her questions about the abuse. Explain the role of investigators (police officer, social worker) and that they are trained to conduct legal investigations. Prepare your child for each step before it occurs by explaining the roles of those in the system. Do not interfere with the investigation.

Partner with the investigator to assure you share what is happening next with your child. Your child benefits from your assurance rather than fearing what might come next with little or no warning. For example, if the investigator says your child will be interviewed by a specialist, you let your child know this is going to happen. Or you explain to your child that he will go to foster care for a brief time during the investigation. Recognizing that this will be very traumatic for your child, you try to reassure your child that this is temporary, and reinforce with child welfare workers the importance of recognizing and addressing your child's fears. You, not the CPS worker or the police, talk with your child. You do not have to tell your child you agree with the action; when the news comes from you, your child will feel more secure.

Abuse-related Legal Cases

These include Criminal, Civil, and Dependency/Child Welfare cases. Cases may proceed concurrently or separately. **Criminal cases** aim to protect the community as well as the child victim. The District Attorney decides whether to file or dismiss charges.

Civil (non-criminal) cases include **custody cases**, **restraining orders**, and **personal injury suits**. Civil cases seek the best interests of the child and/or financial restitution for abuse-related emotional and physical costs. You, as parent or guardian, bring the suit, hire attorneys at your expense (or obtain subsidized legal services), and make decisions about the case. If you cannot protect your child from future abuse due to a familial relationship, the attorney you hire may ask the court for a protective order under the Family Abuse Protection Act, or an Immediate Danger Order as part of a domestic relations/custody proceeding.

Child Welfare cases seek to protect the safety and well-being of a child victim. If evidence exists that your abused child cannot be safe at home because the perpetrator is there, Child Welfare will file a dependency petition to protect your child's safety. Your child may be removed from your home and placed in temporary foster home custody or a children's facility. You may choose to hire an attorney specializing in this complex legal area.

Criminal Cases

States, regions, districts, and counties have specific investigation and trial procedures. We use Oregon procedures as an example and recommend that you obtain information from online sources about your state and locality.

The Report of Abuse is made to Law Enforcement (state police, county sheriffs, city police)

- Office of District Attorney may be informed by Law Enforcement.
- Law Enforcement will often cross-report to Child Welfare, which will initiate a concurrent investigation.
- Law Enforcement or Child Welfare may make a referral to a Child Abuse Assessment Center;

- Child Abuse Assessment Centers were created to reduce the number of interviews and medical evaluations children must undergo. Interviewers are specifically trained in best practices for interviewing child abuse victims. Law Enforcement, Child Welfare, and a non-offending parent are frequently involved.
- Typically, forensic examiners will meet with your child for the assessment. Others may observe through CCTV (closed-caption TV) or mirrored windows.
- Since you are unlikely to be present during the assessment, be sure to ask Assessment Center staff about interviewing and testing procedures so you can explain them to your child.
- A physician may be prohibited from giving an opinion at trial.
- If your child does not disclose penetration, physical evaluation may not be allowed as evidence. Physical evaluations are extremely invasive and should be discussed carefully with the forensic medical provider. *Remember*: It is very difficult for your child to tell anyone, let alone a stranger, about the abuse. Your child is afraid of the person's response and afraid of the consequences of telling.
- Many jurisdictions have services and financial assistance for crime victims. Even if a criminal case is not filed, your child may be entitled to payments from Crime Victims' Assistance funds for costs, such as counseling, reasonably associated with the offense.
- The District Attorney (DA) generally becomes involved when the investigation is completed.
- **The District Attorney reviews the case, determines whether probable cause exists to bring charges, and if so, what charges to bring.**
- **Abuse crimes may either be misdemeanors or felonies, with differing procedures.**
- **Some cases are presented to either a Grand Jury or a Judge at a preliminary hearing.**
- **Once the case is filed, the District Attorney may request an arrest warrant; these are not issued in all cases.**

Grand Juries or preliminary hearings are held in felony cases unless waived by the defendant. The Grand Jury or preliminary hearing determines whether a crime has been committed by the named perpetrator. You or your child may be called as a witness.

- Defendants and defense attorneys are not usually present during Grand Jury proceedings.
- If your jurisdiction holds Preliminary Hearings, both defendant and defense attorney will be present, can cross examine witnesses and present evidence.
- The District Attorney, and if available, Victim's Advocate, help your child feel comfortable testifying.

At Arraignment:

- The defendant is informed of the charges.
- The defendant can apply for court-appointed counsel.
- The judge will briefly review the defendant's constitutional and statutory rights.
- The judge will decide whether to release the defendant conditionally or require him to post bail and for what amount. The defendant will most probably be ordered to have no contact with the victim and the victim's family.
- A Not Guilty plea is almost always entered at arraignment.
- The judge will set additional hearing and motion dates.
- Every jurisdiction has different docketing (scheduling) systems. Familiarize yourself with dockets in your court. You and your child may have the right to be notified of all court appearances, asked about plea negotiations, and speak at certain hearings.
- After arraignment, the Defendant (accused person) and Defense Attorney will conduct their investigation, which can be difficult for victims and their families. Defense investigators frequently contact friends, teachers, counselors, and relatives. You and your child have the right to be informed by the court that you are not required to cooperate with defense investigators/attorneys.

Criminal Trial

- If a case cannot be resolved through plea negotiations, it will be set for trial. The District Attorney aims to prove the charges beyond a reasonable doubt (the weight of evidence suggests the defendant is guilty of the charges).
- Misdemeanor and felony juries may vary in size (6–12 jurors).
- Most criminal cases are resolved through plea negotiation. If the case proceeds to trial, your child and you will probably be required to testify.

Trial Procedures:

- Ask the District Attorney to arrange for your child (victim) to walk through the courtroom, become familiar with the space and types of questions to expect.
- *Voir dire*, selecting a jury, is the first step for a trial. The District Attorney may ask you and your child if you know any of the proposed jurors, and if so, how you know them, and whether you think they would be good jurors for your case. You can attend jury selection though you may not speak. Attorneys are given a limited number of "strikes" to eliminate proposed jurors. Once a jury is agreed upon, it is sworn in, and the judge provides preliminary instructions to the jury.
- The trial begins with opening statements by both attorneys about the case and the evidence.
- Most witnesses may be excluded prior to their testimony. The victim has the right to be present during all trial phases.
- Prosecution witnesses, including victims, are next called to testify. **The District Attorney will question your child** (direct examination), followed by the defense attorney (cross examination). The District Attorney may conclude the examination with redirect examination (**see box below**).[25]
- Witnesses remain under subpoena (legal order to appear) until they are either excused by the court or the trial is concluded. You may be required to remain available for further testimony.

Your child must testify

- If your child had a forensic interview at a Child Abuse Assessment Center, the videotape, along with the testimony, may be admissible in court. However, the *Crawford v Washington* 2004 ruling (541 US 36) determined that the accused has a right to face the accuser, and children in abuse cases are not exempt.
- Crime victims over two-years-old must testify, regardless of whether the alleged crime was sexual.
- Generally, your child must testify in court, with the abuser present, for the taped interview to be admissible as evidence. In some states, a child may be interviewed in the judge's chambers without having to see the accused. In some states, nurses can offer direct testimony; and some allow the first official told by the child to testify as direct evidence.
- Prior to the Crawford ruling, videotaped interviews were admissible, and children's presence was not required in court proceedings.
- **Prosecutors report that the Crawford ruling complicates prosecution of child abusers.**
- Often, children are either unwilling or unable to testify.
- Parents are unwilling for their children to be retraumatized by forcing them to confront their abuser, and to tell their story in a public hearing.
- If your child decides to testify, the Victim Advocate and staff at the Child Abuse Assessment Center can help prepare your child.
- Your child's therapist can help him or her prepare for the perpetrator's presence in court.
- The child's therapist will probably be called as a prosecution witness.

- Defense witnesses testify after prosecution witnesses have testified.
- Both attorneys then make closing arguments.
- In a jury trial, the judge instructs the jury on each charge against the defendant.
- For conviction, judge or jury must find the prosecutor has proved each element of each crime by proof beyond a reasonable doubt.
  - The jury must render a verdict of either guilty or not guilty on some or all charges.
  - When a jury cannot reach a unanimous verdict, the court will declare a mistrial by "hung jury," and the prosecutor can choose to retry the case.
- The District Attorney will notify victims when a verdict has been rendered.
- If a guilty verdict is returned, sentencing may occur immediately following trial or at a later date.

Pre-Sentence Investigations (PSI): Requested by the prosecutor, defense, or judge, they make a sentencing recommendation to the court and are typically completed by the local community corrections office.

Sentencing

- The judge decides an appropriate sentence within rules of sentencing guidelines.
- The judge's sentencing authority is determined by case law, administrative rules and statutes.
- Some felony (more serious) offenses carry a mandatory minimum sentence.
- The defendant's prior history, previous criminal history, pre-sentence evaluations, and Victim Impact Statements inform the judge and assist in sentencing.
- Some convicted defendants may be eligible for probation.
- Some states do not have a parole system.
- The defense attorney may have offered risk assessments and psychological evaluations regarding defendant's risk to the community if on probation as well as treatment that might help

prevent future criminal conduct. The defense may call witnesses to speak to the defendant's character.

- Victims may speak at the sentencing and are allowed to read Victim Impact Statements describing physical, emotional, mental and financial effects of the crime.
- When the victim is a child, you are allowed to write and read a Victim Impact Statement expressing damages your child has suffered.
- Victims or family members may also state their recommended sentence for the defendant.

Victim Impact Statements

- The Statement must contain accurate information about harm done, such as short and long-term physical, psychological, emotional, mental, and relational consequences.
- Relevant medical and psychological reports supporting the statement can be attached.
- Victim Impact Statements can be strongly persuasive during sentencing.
- Victims or family members must advise the District Attorney of their intent to submit a Victim Impact Statement.
- When the victim is a child, you as mother and/or family members can provide a statement.
- Legislation allows Victim Impact Statements to be considered during sentencing of defendants convicted of sexual abuse crimes.
- A victim has the right to information and assistance in preparing the statement.
- The Victim Impact Statement may be written by the victim, written by the victim with help from someone else, written by a counselor working with a victim, or prepared by a qualified person designated by the prosecutor.

- The Statement relates to the personal harm suffered as a direct result of the offense.
- The victim chooses whether to make a Victim Impact Statement. No one may make a statement on behalf of a victim if the victim objects.
- The victim is entitled to read the Statement to the court.
- The court may accept and consider the Victim Impact Statement at any time after the conviction and before sentencing the offender.
- The court may not interpret the victim's not making a Statement as the victim not having suffered harm.
- See the "Victim Impact Page" on www.mosac.net for additional information.

Victim Rights

Through state laws, crime victims have basic and fundamental rights, including the right to be informed of rights and services at the earliest possible time. In some states, Law Enforcement provides victims with a list of rights, talks with them about their rights, and provides phone numbers for support and advocacy. Victim rights include the right to:

- Be notified and informed;
- Be present;
- Be heard;
- Be protected;
- Receive compensation and restitution;
- Have a Victim Advocate present;
- Obtain records;
- Additional rights for child victims and dependent persons;
- Speedy disposition of a case.

See the "Victim Rights" page at www.mosac.net.

Criminal case appeals

- Include a review of the trial and the defendant's effort to justify reversal of the conviction or reduction of sentence;
- Can be lengthy and complex since several courts might eventually review the case;
- Can take years to complete;
- See "Appeals: What Victims Should Know About the Appeals Process" at www.mosac.net

Civil Cases

Monetary compensation is sought for damages resulting from the sexual abuse your child suffered. If the criminal case was dismissed by the prosecutor for lack of evidence, a civil case may impose consequences on the offender. You must hire civil case attorneys to sue the offender/perpetrator and any organization that failed to protect your child from abuse.

Civil cases also include divorce and custody cases, restraining orders and personal injury suits.

Child Welfare (Dependency) Cases

Child welfare agencies investigate child safety issues and risk of harm to children, including whether the non-offending parent can provide a safe home. Investigations may be:

- **Founded**: Sufficient evidence exists to believe your child has been neglected or abused. If you as a non-offending parent can protect your child from the abuser, the case is unlikely to be entered as founded.
- **Unfounded**: Evidence was not adequate to conclude your child has been or is at risk of abuse; or although your child was abused, an ongoing risk of abuse is not determined. Child Welfare will close an unfounded case. The criminal case may still proceed.
- **Unable to determine**: the investigation did not provide not enough information to decide whether your child is or has been at risk of abuse. This does not mean abuse did not occur. DHS may not have been able to interview everyone in the case.

A decision to remove your child from your home may occur when
- The abuser cannot be arrested and refuses to leave your home;
- An unsupportive mother is angry at her child;
- Domestic violence or substance abuse exists in the home;
- The home is not "minimally adequate" to meet a child's needs; or
- Your child requests removal from the home.

If your child appears to be in *immediate danger*, Child Welfare or, infrequently, Law Enforcement, will remove your child from your home through a voluntary safety plan agreement between you and the agency without court involvement. If your child's safety cannot be assured, a Dependency Petition, will be filed with the court stating the reasons for removal. A Dependency Petition does not **require** removal of your child from your home.

Court hearings are then held.
- The court will often appoint an attorney for the parents and the children, for the dependency petition only.
- The attorney for your child represents the child and is not your attorney.
- Sometimes the child's attorney advocates for your child's best interests, and sometimes for what the child wants.
- Some jurisdictions will also appoint a Court Appointed Special Advocate (CASA) to conduct investigations and report what actions are in your child's best interests.
- Some jurisdictions may appoint a Guardian Ad Litem (GAL) for a child in addition to or instead of the lawyer and the CASA.
- You may be required to repay the State for both the cost of attorneys as well as contributing to the costs associated with substitute care.
- Child Welfare is required to try to notify parents about the date, time and location of all hearings. The court can and will proceed with a hearing even if the parents are not present.

A **Shelter Care Hearing** is usually the first hearing after a child is placed in substitute care and a petition is filed with the court.

- This hearing will determine whether your child will remain in shelter care until the trial on the Dependency Petition.
- Parents have the right to a trial on the petition allegations.
- Federal Law (the Adoption and Safe Families ACT—ASFA) requires a Dependency Petition to be adjudicated within 60 days of the date of removal.

Dependency Trial

- The burden of proof typically lies with the Child Welfare Agency.
- You or your child may have to testify at this trial.
- The parties often agree to a settlement allowing the court to take jurisdiction without going through trial.
- The judge will make your child a ward of the court and require certain services to ensure your child can be safely returned home.

Dispositional Hearing: All parties provide information regarding the case plan and services requested so the child may be reintegrated into your home.

If your child is the subject of a dependency/child protection case, we strongly recommend you hire an attorney with expertise in this legal specialty.

Legal Terminology information is available on www.mosac.net.

Legal and emotional considerations if your child discloses as an adult

If your child discloses as an adult (defined by the respective state), he or she is responsible to bring any legal action. The ability to bring criminal and/or civil charges will depend on the statute of limitations in the state of residence as a child. Your adult child's emotions and need for your belief, support and efforts to offer emotional and/or actual protection are equivalent to those of a minor child. **Do *not* make the mistake of thinking, "my child is an adult and can handle this emotionally as an adult."** Your adult child is feeling the emotions she or he felt and was unable to express as a child. She needs your belief, support and protection now. The disclosure of child sexual abuse in adulthood has the same potential for fracturing your family, precipitating a crisis for you, and changing your life as does the experience when your child is under eighteen. Even if your adult child is living outside your home, his need for your support is very strong. The difficulty of separating from your child's father, if he is your husband or partner, can be extreme, especially when you are no longer young. Though an adult, your child needs your unwavering support. Failing to give and demonstrate it can result in a deep and possibly unbridgeable rift between you.

What is expected of mothers during legal action involving sexual abuse of your minor child?

During your child's evaluation and law enforcement investigation, you will be asked for family history:

- Current family status (housing, employment, family sleeping arrangements, daily routines);
- Family violence;
- Substance abuse;
- History of sexual behaviors;
- History of mental health services;
- Family psychological health;
- Your child's history (birth, development, health, education, prior trauma, social skills, emotional problems);
- Your child's behavioral problems, particularly warning signs of sexual abuse.

Warning signs of sexual abuse can confirm sexual abuse allegations. When you talk with professionals evaluating your child, be as detailed and thorough as possible about physical, emotional, and behavioral signs you have observed. We suggest you review **Physical, Behavioral and Emotional Warning Signs in Chapter 2**.

The more severe the warning signs, the more likely abuse has occurred. A cluster of warning signs suggests your child is experiencing severe distress, and abuse has most likely occurred.

When the abuser is a family member, **DHS/Child Welfare will probably evaluate your appropriateness as a safe parent for your sexually**

abused child and your other children. The most complex circumstances include the abuser as your partner; suspicion you did not protect your child's safety and/or allowed the abuser access to your child following knowledge that abuse occurred; and your emotional instability during the child abuse assessment. You may also have a history of child sexual abuse, increasing the likelihood of PTSD, depression, and dissociation interfering with effective parenting during this crisis.

Most child sexual abuse situations are very complex. You must mother your abused child and other children; deal with your feelings; cope with the perpetrator and other family members; and manage during the investigation and legal case. The crisis that begins at disclosure may last a very long time; its impact may never end. Your child or children will suffer ongoing consequences from the abuse, and your relationship with the abuser may be destroyed.

While all these major stressors are interacting, you will be required to make decisions about the abuser moving out, and preventing contact between the abuser and your child. Professionals may judge you as non-supportive. You may be blamed for the child's abuse and accused of having known about it. Your child victim may also believe at a deep psychological level that you knew or should have known, based on signs your child thought you saw. The abuser may have told your child you knew about the abuse. If you defend yourself, defend the perpetrator, argue with DHS, or are angry with either Law Enforcement or DHS, you will be perceived as "part of the problem."

In an opposite scenario, you may have previously seen sexual abuse signs and insisted to DHS that abuse occurred. If the case was not founded, you may now be considered to be a "problem." Whether you defend or blame the abuser, your responses may be considered inappropriate, you may be perceived as potentially unstable, and consideration may be given to removal of your child from your care.[26]

Appropriate anger may be misinterpreted as manipulation and dishonesty. You are often in a double bind, blamed for action or inaction. This feels like a no-win situation. **You must have reliable support and counseling**.

Disclosure may have occurred after your child's father left your home and you initiated divorce proceedings. Your child may now feel safe enough to disclose abuse. The allegation may be interpreted as a fabrication to convince the court about child custody. Law Enforcement, DHS, and court systems often do not respond supportively to mothers during divorce and/or custody proceedings. You may find yourself in an additional double bind. **In these very complex and challenging circumstances, we highly recommend hiring a knowledgeable, competent, well-respected attorney and assuring you are in counseling with a trustworthy, informed and capable therapist.**

Remember: Children rarely lie about abuse. The consequences of telling are too painful. Betrayal bonds maintain attachment to the abuser and may preclude the victim's disclosing abuse.

The relationship you establish with professionals and agency representatives is crucial to the ongoing investigation. You must monitor your emotional responses. Overemotional responses (hysteria or extreme rage at perpetrator) and lack of emotional response (overly calm and detached, cold) will both be judged negatively.

You may have very strong fight or flight fantasies about killing the abuser, running away with your child, or even harming yourself or ending your life to get away from your severe pain. **Do not act on these!** Your child needs you! Recognize that these fantasies reflect feelings of frustration and rage at a time of extreme crisis. Recognize the source of your feelings and focus your **actions** on helping your child and yourself.

Many professionals continue to blame mothers, believing that mothers must have known about the abuse and did not protect their child. Although research has consistently shown that most mothers did not know about the abuse prior to the disclosure,[27] mother-blaming continues. Mothers often do not receive support from professionals, and their grieving is not acknowledged. To survive the investigation and legal process, you must find support from friends, family members, victim advocates, and trustworthy professionals. You can stay strong by focusing on and communicating your belief, support and protection to your child. Some mothers are sustained by faith, others by membership in support groups, and still others by trusting their instincts and strengths in tough times.

Coping with the court verdict

The end of the trial and/or sentencing is **not** the end of its effects on you and your child. If the offender is convicted and is a family member, you may feel grief and rage. If the offender plea bargained, you may be disappointed at the outcome. If the offender is acquitted, you may feel angry, afraid, or sad. Post-trial support services are available. Reassure your child victim that the court outcome, if dismissal, acquittal, or plea bargain, does **not** mean the abuser is innocent. The court did not have sufficient evidence to impose a more severe punishment.[28] This is emotional for you, your child and family.

After the trial, family, friends, and acquaintances may ask your child for details about the case. While the trial usually ends the criminal charge, a family court case may still be open. Politely request family and friends not to ask invasive questions.

When the legal outcome is not what you want

Face the **reality** of current legal systems and outcomes. When your child's biological father is the perpetrator, if there was not enough evidence to charge him, he will be free, and you may have minimal legal recourse in custody disputes, resulting in his continued access to your child. This will add fear, anxiety, frustration, anger, helplessness, and horror to your emotions.

Knowing this possibility in advance, you may not want to report or pursue legal action. For your child's sake, proceed. You are looking out for his or her best interests. Although you may not win initially, you must keep fighting for your child's safety. Even if only you and your child know you are doing your best, this is still very important to your child's mental health. The current legal system is what we have, with its flaws, inequities, misunderstandings of sexual abuse and family dynamics, and sometimes uninformed professionals. Be a voice. Speak up about your experience, and work towards change for other children and mothers. The **Appendix** includes advocacy resources. Think of #MeToo as a role model for child sexual abuse advocacy. There is strength in numbers. Changes in unfair laws do happen as a result of informed advocacy.

Reality Check: If your child was abused by her biological parent, you may have to face your inability to protect your child. You may have to *surrender* your child to the perpetrator for unsupervised or overnight or weekend visits, causing you heart- and gut-wrenching pain. Expect to feel anxiety, fear and possibly panic before and during your child's visitation with the perpetrator. At future status hearings, the court will assess whether you are cooperating rather than negatively influencing your child against his biological parent. The court will not see the risk and danger as you see it. This is a frequent outcome. In current systems, despite danger to children, reunification is the goal.

Keep records of your child's behavior before and after visits with the perpetrator. Always have someone with you as a witness at these times. Keep talking with your child. Make your home the peaceful, safe, secure sanctuary your child needs. If your child has been abused, even if the abuse does not recur during visits, your child's brain has been wired to sense danger and experience fear and anxiety; symptoms may follow visits. Track these, and make sure your child's therapist is aware of emotional and behavioral symptoms prior to and following visits. Keep your child in therapy for the long haul. And remain in therapy yourself. You will need support and a place to deal with your feelings. You may also find "Coping with Unconfirmed Cases," and the Facebook Chat Room at www.mosac.net helpful. You are not powerless! Think of yourself as empowered and find ways to use your power as positively as possible.

CHAPTER SUMMARY

This chapter discussed legal action after reports of child sexual abuse. We emphasized the critically important, and very difficult role that you, your child's mother, must play in navigating through these complex systems. In **Chapter 5**, we'll discuss how you can continue to support your child going forward. The **Appendix** includes advocacy resources.

Support for You and Your Child

I'm Desperate. I Need Someone to Talk with Who Has Survived This

Often others cannot understand, cannot know the feelings, the horror, the grief you are experiencing. It is as if someone in a safe home in central Kansas is trying to understand the feelings of someone standing on the Pacific Coast amidst recent tsunami destruction—their home swept away, their family hurt or lost.

Overview

Child sexual abuse has lifelong impact. Immediate and long-term support is essential. Your emotional and physical health are key in supporting your abused child.

Remember: Maternal support is the best predictor of your child's recovery from abuse.

Barriers to obtaining support

You may feel isolated. You may not know anyone else in your circumstances. You may never have talked to anyone about sexual abuse or be uncomfortable talking about sex to others. You may have little or no knowledge about sexual abuse, warning signs, behaviors of sex offenders, the victimization process, or family dynamics after disclosure of sexual abuse.

Secrecy surrounds sexual abuse. Once the "secret code" has been broken, you may feel shunned, excluded and shamed. Sexual abuse is called the silent epidemic because it *is* an epidemic about which few speak.

In addition to these barriers, your initial reactions, such as shock, denial, anger, guilt, fear, anxiety, grief, and possibly depression, may prevent you from talking about it. You may not want to ask for help or talk about the abuse. Your own ambivalence increases the sense of isolation. How can you tell others, share a story, or ask for support when part of you is not sure you believe it happened? Or if you are not sure what to do? At the time that you most need support, you may be least likely to seek it.

Now the secret is out. You are telling the appropriate authorities and doing everything you can to protect your child. You will hold this knowledge for the rest of your life. You will choose whom you tell about it. Your decisions will be based on the safety and protection of your child and assuring your safety and support.

Your ability to trust has been damaged by this trauma. If the perpetrator is someone with whom you thought you had a close, trusting relationship, the violation of trust is significant. People, friends, family, and the world may feel much less safe now.

Pay attention to your needs for support and seek support from people with whom you feel comfortable, whom you trust, who do not judge or criticize you, and who listen and validate your and your child's feelings. Keep reaching out!

This chapter assists you in gathering resources and building a support system.

Supports include:

1. **Professionals:** Mental health providers, therapy groups, and your physician;

2. **Family:** Safe family members;

3. **Friends:** Those who understand your distress, grief, and family damage;

4. **Community members:** Your physician; spiritual and faith leaders; crisis workers; and mentors who are comfortable and/or experienced with child sexual abuse;

5. **Local support groups:** Peer-led support groups for mothers of sexually abused children; Al-Anon, Codependents Anonymous and Adult Children of Alcoholics and Dysfunctional Families (ACA);

6. **Online support groups for mothers of sexually abused children**: These include grief, codependence and addiction groups (**See Appendix**);
7. **Recognizing and managing your stress**: Effective coping strategies help you mother your child and manage challenges;
8. **Lifestyle changes**: Increased attention to self-care and balance to help you and your child deal with grief and recovery. You are also your own support resource!

Support Options

1. Mental Health and Health Professionals

Many mothers of sexually abused children experience **Posttraumatic Stress Disorder (PTSD)**, significant **depression, anxiety or panic**. PTSD is caused by a traumatic event outside the normal range of experience. Symptoms can continue for weeks, months, or years. You may reexperience events mentally and in nightmares, review them obsessively while feeling powerless, helpless and hopeless. Support is essential to prevent or reduce depression and PTSD from affecting your ability to mother your children. Children also may have PTSD, depression, and anxiety.

Mothers and child victims can benefit from therapy. Professional mental health providers include **trained counselors, clinical social workers, psychologists and psychiatrists. Individual therapy** can provide a safe place to deal with your emotional and practical issues. Effective and trustworthy therapy builds communication skills, assertiveness, and abuse prevention knowledge.

Choose a therapist carefully! Check the therapist's education and credentials; ask questions about training, experience with child sexual abuse and family systems; avoid mother-blaming attitudes.

Remember: You are choosing and hiring a therapist with whom you must be comfortable. Be sure a therapist is qualified and a good fit; try to interview at least two.

As soon as possible, your **child can begin therapy** with a trustworthy therapist experienced in assessing and treating child victims. Your child will tell her story of the abuse and may draw pictures of her thoughts and feelings. She will learn new coping skills. You will consult with the therapist about how best to support your child at home. Occasional sessions with you and your child can help with your relationship. Your child may be angry, believing you knew and did not protect her. Your child's belief in your support is integral to her recovery.

Your **child's physician** can provide necessary legal documentation of appointments and your child's sexual abuse symptoms. Sign an authorization allowing communication between your child's therapist and physician. **Your physician** may also help you with your emotional and physical reactions to your child's sexual abuse.

Therapy groups for mothers are usually available in an agency or therapist's office, facilitated by a therapist specializing in child sexual abuse or a sex offender treatment provider offering family therapy. Child Protective Services (CPS) may also require you to attend **group therapy**. Sharing feelings with an experienced therapist and other mothers can be helpful. Therapy groups can also teach assertiveness, anger and stress management, cognitive-behavior therapy, mindfulness, communication, parenting skills, and creative expression.

2. Family

Disclosure of child sexual abuse is traumatizing and life-altering for family members. They will experience shock, grief, worry, concern for the child, mother and father. When abuse is perpetrated by a stranger or community member, family and friends may generously help and support mothers and victims. When your partner is not the abuser, lean on each other and support one another in childcare and legal actions. If you are a single parent, look to friends you can trust to help you.

When the disclosed abuse was incest (sexual activity between family members), trauma, damaged trust, conflicting feelings, pain and distress increase. You will experience more intense emotions. All family members will struggle.

Prepare yourself for a range of family dynamics when the abuser is a family member:

- Pressure not to report the abuse;
- Family rifts;

- Side-taking;
- Anger;
- Comments about the abuse in the abused child's presence;
- Some family members believing the abuser's denial.

Remember: Family members will move through grief, shock and denial. Some will make hurtful comments to discourage your child from speaking out or cause recanting.

Inappropriate comments include:

- She's ruined for life.
- The monster should be killed.
- How could you not have known about the abuse?
- She probably just made it up.
- Why do you think he would tell a story like that about his father?
- He'll get over it quickly.
- She won't remember.
- Poor child.
- How horrible.
- She probably brought it on herself.

Be careful; be selective about *whom to tell*. **Do not** keep abuse secret because you fear family members' reactions. If the abuser is a family member, **all** parents in the family need to know, as their children may be at risk or already be victims. A father-figure abuser will leave your home. If he has not been arrested, other family members may help him. When the abuse was perpetrated by your partner, your emotions are overwhelming. When the abuse was perpetrated by a sibling, you will struggle with how to love and support both children. Your struggle is compounded by the family's frequent inability to offer emotional support. It can feel as if an atomic bomb hit your family. What was familiar, dependable, and comforting has been blown away.

Be mindful in allowing your child to spend time with family members. Be assertive in setting boundaries: ask others to speak privately with you and not comment in your child's presence. Consider avoiding those who are toxic for you and/or your child.

Reality Check when the abuse is incest—sexual abuse by a parent or parental figure:

- Many family members will be angry that you reported the abuse, preferring to resolve the problem *in* the family without legal or social services involvement. Standing against this resistance is difficult; you may be ambivalent as well. "Don't Talk, Don't Trust, Don't Feel" may be an unspoken inter-generational family rule. **Identify those family members who will support you and avoid others.**

- The most egregious forms of betrayal may occur following a sexual abuse disclosure. If the perpetrator has been violent to you, intimidation, fear, helplessness and anxiety can cause difficulty in acting firmly and protectively. You and your child may need to move to a safe house for protection during this vulnerable time. Seek help quickly and implement an Emergency Plan to keep yourself and your child safe (**See Chapter 6**).

- Suspicion and mistrust will increase. Other changes will occur in family relationships; traditions, holidays and celebrations; boundaries, demonstration of affection; and childcare decisions.

When the abuser was the biological father, stepfather, or boyfriend, social services or treatment providers may present a family reunification plan, based on the perpetrator's successful completion of treatment. **Re-abuse risk increases when the perpetrator returns to your home.**[29] Special safety precautions are necessary with a thoughtfully developed and implemented Safety Plan to avoid further abuse (**see Chapter 6**).

Influences preventing family members from responding helpfully:

- **Denial:** The disclosure may initially be unbelievable. Grandparents do not believe their child could do this to their grandchild. Relatives take sides. Divorce and custody actions or domestic violence restraining orders may be underway.

- **Fear:** Family members fear consequences to the perpetrator and damage to the family's reputation.

- **Grief:** In their pain, loss, and mourning, family members may be unable to reach out emotionally to you and your child.

- **Anger:** At the perpetrator, at you for not protecting your child or for being perceived as complicit in the abuse, or at the victim, saying that she is "making it up" or angry that he or she is "blowing up" the family.

- **Beliefs about privacy and family secrets:** Children may be taught you don't talk to anyone about what happens inside the home. Telling, talking about, and reporting abuse are all secrecy code violations.

- **Inadequate knowledge and information about sexual abuse:** Many people simply do not know about or understand sexual abuse and its consequences. They may be unable to imagine or embarrassed about it.

- **Ambivalence:** Family members may want to believe the perpetrator and the victim. They may love all family members, yet be confused and irrational in demanding to protect the perpetrator at the expense of the victim. Their ambivalence may result in shifting or nonexistent support for you and your child.

- **Trust:** They may trust the abuser's apparent persuasive presentation and respect his high community stature. Offenders are skilled manipulators who can groom family members as well as victims.

- **Perception the victim isn't suffering and is fine:** Victims may have been abused for years and have developed coping and survival skills such as dissociation and may not appear seriously distressed. Acting out by older children or adolescent victims may reduce their credibility, suggesting lying or ulterior motives. These doubts and judgments may affect your ability to believe, support and protect your child victim.

- **Lack of empathy and compassion:** Family members may be unable to understand your and your child's overwhelming emotions, or to reach out.

- **Minimizing consequences of the abuse:** Family members may believe abuse does not cause long-term damage, an unfortunately persisting myth.

- **Other abusers in the family:** Child sexual abuse, particularly incest, often crosses generations; grandparents, uncles and cousins may be abusers or abuse victims. Abusers are unlikely to support your child victim's account.

Remember: Sexual abuse occurs when *opportunity* is present. Some **suggestions to manage family communication**:

- Protect your child's privacy.
- Disclose abuse details to professionals only.
- Make sure your child knows which family members you have told about the abuse.
- Ask family members not to talk to other people about the abuse.
- Be direct and firm in responding to questions.
- Make your limits in sharing information clear.
- Directly state you do not want to talk about it.

Family members may not know *how* to communicate effectively. Some families discourage open expression of feelings, believing in *mind-reading*, that others know what they think and feel, and they can tell what another person is thinking or feeling. However, mind-reading is **not** possible. Listening to and talking with another person is the only solution.

Signs of ineffective family communication:

- Angry outbursts;
- Arguments and fights;
- Escaping into television, social media, sleeping more than usual;
- Few family activities;
- Few family meals;
- Isolating in bedrooms;
- Spending time away from home;
- Increased use of alcohol and other mind-altering substances.

Family members in survival mode may isolate, avoid communicating, or attack and blame each other. You and your children experience torn loyalties, guilt, and confusion. With your attention focused on your abused child, siblings may feel neglected. Effective communication can reduce many of these problems.

Remember: Family members may know nothing about sexual abuse, or they may have seen a movie or read an article or book. They usually do not have any true awareness of your experience or your child's experience, unless they have experienced it themselves.

Healthy communication skills can be learned. Respect is key to success.
- Focus on solutions, not problems;
- Don't blame or attack the other person;
- Use "I" statements, saying what you think, feel, want, or need;
- Intentionally *listen* to the other person, so you can understand him or her;
- Manage your own emotions;
- Be mindful; stay in the present, noticing and paying attention to what is happening *now*;
- Family therapy facilitated by a therapist in a safe environment may be helpful to you and extended family members.

Siblings

Open communication is essential for a healthy family environment. Your children must feel safe in talking about the sexual abuse and their feelings. You also must ask your children direct questions about whether others have abused them or other siblings. Do not make assumptions. If a sibling denies being abused, **do not** reject the possibility. **Some siblings do not disclose until years later**. They may have known about the abuse and kept the secret because of fear, shame or inability to know how or whom to tell; they may also have been victims. Lack of communication adds to already-present pain.

Siblings' needs are often not viewed as urgent. Siblings may be neglected while you are attending to the reporting and legal action following the victim's disclosure. Siblings may be struggling with guilt, shame, and self-blame. If the abuser is a sibling, he may also be a victim acting out sexually with others. These possibilities compound the complexity of issues that mothers face as you attempt to rebuild a safe and protective environment for *all* children. Parenting recommendations are included in "Positive Parenting as a MOSAC," in **Chapter 6**.

3. Friends

Sexual abuse is overlaid with false beliefs, fear, shame, and judgment. Friends may not know what to say or how to help. They may act as if nothing has happened or distance themselves from you. What happened to you could happen to them. They fear their children could be abused. Abuse feels too close to their own homes. Friends may avoid you when you need them the most.

Telling your friends you need help will lead you to those most willing and able to walk with you now. Friends can accompany you to interviews and court dates; help with childcare during scheduled appointments; be with you to talk and cry; encourage you and help you stay strong.

Be careful how you approach friends other than those you genuinely trust. A good rule of thumb is to share a little and then closely observe the person's reaction and response. Pay attention to your feelings about their response. Right now, you, not they, are the one who needs support. Friends do not always understand mental health conditions or how to respond to friends' symptoms. They may give you unhelpful advice and suggestions. Rely on your counselor and physician for professional support and your trustworthy friends for moral support.

4. Community Members

Spiritual and faith advisors, crisis workers, and mentors can help. The local women's crisis center can offer emergency shelter and services for mothers and sexually abused children. DHS can help with food, temporary housing, and transportation. You may need childcare help. Your Victim Advocacy Center will offer information about Crime Victim Compensation funds to cover costs of medical, mental health services and related financial needs.

5. Local Support Groups

Support groups are member-led, offering a sense of belonging where you feel less "alone," have a safe place to talk about feelings and gain needed emotional support. Groups are effective because members are other mothers whose experiences and feelings are similar to yours. To find a local support group, ask the Victim Advocate, Women's Crisis Center, Child Abuse Assessment Center, and local therapists knowledgeable about child sexual abuse.

Reality Check: relatively few local therapy and support groups are available for mothers. Larger cities, with mental health agencies specializing in child abuse, are more likely to offer these groups.

Other self-help groups such as Recovery International, Codependents Anonymous, Al-Anon and Adult Children of Alcoholics (ACA)/ Dysfunctional Families may be helpful. Some offer mentors, individuals further along the path of recovery.

6. Online Support Groups

These may be found on websites for mothers. Some are confidential, requiring approval and sign-in; others are public. Some groups and a confidential Chat Group are available through the MOSAC website (**see Appendix also**). Be aware that information posted on social media can be shared.

7. Recognize and Manage Stress

Acute stress can become chronic (ongoing), changing your brain chemistry and lowering your immune response. Effective coping helps avoid serious mental, emotional, and physical difficulties. Improving your quality of life can build resilience, enhance your immune system and increase your resistance to illness.

We sometimes forget self-care when we feel overwhelmed. Attend to your physical, mental, and spiritual needs to help you stay healthy, present and supportive to your child, and minimize negative psychological and physical effects.

Your goal is to cope **effectively**. **Avoid negative coping strategies** that make things worse, such as:

• Increased alcohol consumption;
• Use and abuse of other mood-altering drugs;
• Uncontrolled anger;
• Untreated or unmanaged depression;
• Gambling;
• Looking for validation from new partners.

Eat regular meals, exercise regularly, and decrease use of substances (caffeine, alcohol, cigarettes, drugs) that blunt your anxiety without truly reducing it. Instead walk with a friend, work out, write in a journal, meditate, or use other healthy coping strategies described below to reduce stress.

You can:

- **Build relationships** with friends and community supports;
- **View crisis as a** *challenge*, not a horrible situation that you cannot endure;
- **Practice acceptance** of the reality of the abuse and its effects on your child;
- **Set realistic goals**; make a to-do list for today and this week. Accomplishing small goals helps you feel more in charge;
- **Engage in positive, active decision-making to solve problems**, reduce feelings of helplessness and powerlessness and increase feelings of accomplishment;
- **Be gentle and kind**, not self-judging or self-blaming;
- **Keep perspective**; tomorrow is a new day. Life will eventually be less chaotic and painful. Practice *Beginner's Mind*;
- **Take care of yourself**; take a bubble bath or go to the beach or museum. Do something new and enjoyable; renew yourself;
- **Enhance your spirituality**. Read, pray, meditate, go to your place of worship.

Additional coping strategies include:

- **Mindfulness:** Paying attention to the present moment without judgment, staying focused and aware. Mindfulness can be applied to every life activity, such as eating and walking mindfully. Mindfulness helps to reduce stress and improve coping, concentration, relaxation, self-esteem, self-acceptance and compassion.
- **Healthy diet:** Improves your energy, health and mood. A consistent family mealtime is helpful.
- **Exercise:** Increases energy, protects health and reduces fatigue from stress.
- **Sleep routine:** Calms and restores the body, improves concentration and mood, and increases your ability to manage stress.
- **Meditation:** Quiets your body, mind, and emotions, increases relaxation, focus, and awareness, reduces stress, improves the

immune system, and increases overall health. Meditation is to the mind what physical exercise is to the body. Meditation may be sitting, walking, or standing; yoga is a well-known meditation.

- **Breathing exercises:** Focusing on your breath and breathing deeply can help calm you.
- **Assertiveness:** Assertive responses are thoughtful and planned, not impulsive and emotional. Using rational rather than emotional responses to interpersonal conflict increases self-confidence and mutual respect.
- **Positive self-talk:** Focus on positive feelings and thoughts.
- **Coping skills:** CBT (Cognitive Behavioral Therapy) and DBT (Dialectical Behavioral Therapy) teach helpful skills for use in difficult situations.
- **Music:** Is healing and can alter emotions. Release emotions through movement or sing away sadness.
- **Journaling:** Reduces stress, promotes creativity and increases healing. Write your thoughts and feelings; release anger and pain.
- **Poetry:** Write in whatever form you choose.
- **Prayer:** Helps to release worry, stress, anxiety, and fear.
- **Recreation:** Helps release stress, increasing health, positive attitudes and enjoyment. Recreation *re-creates* you. Enjoy arts and crafts, read, view a film, visit a zoo or children's museum. Creative recreation will also model positive coping strategies for your children.
- **Helping others:** Reaching out to other moms and others in your community provides mutual support and helps you feel better.

Remember: Humor is healing! Laughter is good medicine for everyone, releasing mood-elevating endorphins in your body.

8. Lifestyle Changes

Your sexually abused child has been traumatized; you, a secondary trauma victim, must cope with the aftermath. Daily routines will change. You and your children may move, perhaps near supportive family members. Your children may change schools. Friendships may shift. You may not have either energy or time to maintain full-time employment and meet therapeutic and legal appointments. Your state may have family medical leave. Explore your options.

Moving past your fears to seek support can be very difficult. Sexual abuse is not easy to discuss; you realistically fear not being believed or understood, being blamed, hearing hurtful comments, or others aligning with the abuser. These outcomes sometimes occur. Do not let fear keep you isolated and alone.

Developing resources and support, and practicing self-care and stress management, will help you move successfully through this life crisis. You need to stay strong for your children!

CHAPTER SUMMARY

In this chapter, we discussed specific supports for you and your child including obtaining trustworthy professional help; family, friends, community, local and online support groups, stress management and lifestyle changes. **Chapter 6** will address parenting as a MOSAC and skill-building with your child.

CHAPTER 6

Parenting as a MOSAC

Overview

This chapter addresses parenting as a MOSAC and skill-building with your child.

Post-disclosure parenting is challenging. While you are coping with your reactions to your child's abuse, all family members continue to need your love and care. You will be torn by conflicting emotions when the victim and your other children most need you. Your child's needs must take precedence; to best parent your child, you must deal effectively with your emotions. Your loving response and support are the foundation for your child's healing.

Imagine your child's feelings: something horrific, frightening and confusing has happened to him. If you no longer look or act like the calm, attentive caring mother he knew; or you look angry, anxious, or panicky, he will feel worse. Do your best to keep your emotions in check except when alone or with safe support. Your child also needs continued assurance that she is **not** responsible in any way for what happened to her. Notice whether she is blaming herself.

Your child must know you believe, support, will protect her, and are not angry about her disclosure. If your child perceives these are lacking or that you are extremely distressed, he may recant or change his account of abuse. Your child can sense your emotions nonverbally. You must control your emotions and seek support for yourself.

When the sexual abuse was perpetrated by a family member, your child may have confused feelings towards you. He or she may:

- Blame you for not preventing or stopping the abuse;
- Be angry, believing you knew about the abuse and let it happen;
- Feel you "should" have known about the abuse and did not;
- Feel betrayed by you;
- Lose trust in you;
- Be afraid that, because of the abuse, you will be upset or angry at them;
- Fear your rejection if they tell and you do not appear to believe them;
- Be angry at you if they feel you do not believe them;
- Feel neglected and alone if you do not notice their hurt, negative thoughts and feelings related to the abuse;
- Feel disappointed you didn't get their "clues" about being abused;
- No longer believe you are a good parent, with loss of communication and effective parenting.

Talk with your child. Be patient, calm, supportive. And seek help in family therapy.

Remember: Abusers lie to victims.

- The perpetrator may have told your child you knew, said it was okay, or did not care.
- The perpetrator was someone your child trusted, who betrayed that trust; your child now is no longer trusting.
- Your child is a victim of a crime that can affect her throughout her life.
- Your support is one of the best predictors of her recovery.

You need a special skill-set to parent a sexually abused child. You must support your child gently, with empathy, availability, and careful listening. Think about your child's helplessness and powerlessness to prevent or stop the abuse. Your child needs to feel competent and empowered in decision-making to regain self-esteem, feel safe, and reduce fear. Offering choices and responsibilities in daily life will increase her sense of control. Inform him about future events and decisions, and encourage him to express his thoughts and feelings, knowing they are heard and valued.

You and your child can learn communication and expressive skills through online or in-person classes for parents of traumatized children.

Therapists for sexually abused children can teach skills you can share with your child.

Reality Check: Child Protective Services (CPS) may evaluate your competence to parent. While this may seem unfair, the system is designed to assure protection for children. Sometimes mothers do not report or protect. CPS will assess your:

- Denial or ambivalence regarding your child's disclosure;
- Ability to put your child's needs first and to provide stable parenting;
- Empathy for and ability to protect your child;
- Parenting skills in daily life, such as routine, structure, discipline, consistency, and support of your child's education and continuing development;
- Personal stability, independence, assertiveness, mental and physical health, sexual abuse history, addictions or unhealthy relationships.

Positive Parenting

Provide a positive, safe environment for your child to heal. Your mothering will comfort your child, help him or her feel more secure, able to recover from the sexual abuse, develop healthy habits and interrelationship skills, and grow up to be a healthy adult.

How to respond:

- Provide **consistent, predictable love and care**, offering ample opportunity for your child to share her thoughts and feelings;
- When setting **boundaries**, reassure your child that you love him, and that boundaries are for his safety. Maintain boundaries, even under pressure;
- When **negative child behaviors** occur, observe, respond, and discuss these with your child. Ask your child to participate in setting consequences for specific behaviors;
- **Do not personalize.** This is not about you. When your child's moods go up and down, remind yourself that your child is in pain;

- **If your child blames you, do *not* defend yourself. Listen. Love. Detach. This will help your child learn to trust you again;**
- Be an **"emotional container"** for your child who feels overwhelmed. Trauma has caused them to develop beliefs and expectations about themselves, adults, and the world that affect their emotions. We are an emotional container for them when we respond calmly, help them express negative beliefs and learn they are safe, capable, and lovable;
- **Remain calm.** If your child explodes, remain calm. If your child is out of control, remain calm. This benefits you both;
- Teach your child **coping skills**, with the help of her therapist. You can also learn about self-soothing skills that help your child calm herself. These may include mindfulness, breathing, relaxation, yoga, music and art.
- **Pay attention** to the books, television shows, and movies your child watches. Limit your child's exposure to programs that might increase anxiety or nightmares.
- **Accept that your child does not understand why or what she is saying or doing.** She is in pain and striking out. You are probably her closest and safest person and a trustworthy target. Again, don't personalize. It is not about you.
- **Do not allow your child to hit or endanger you.** Talk calmly with your child and acknowledge her painful feelings.
- **If your child acts out sexually,** he may be trying to meet needs previously met during sexual abuse. Although sexual abuse may involve pain and force, often love, caring, and intimacy seem present. Touch, affection, and nurturing, although abusive, may also have been comforting. This comfort now is missing. You must of course prevent acting out toward other children or with adults. Be aware of your child's need for increased physical comfort and affection.

Sexually abused children benefit from structure, consistency, guidelines and rules at home. Rules should be clear, explained prior to expecting they are followed, and consequences clearly stated. Rules should apply at home and elsewhere.

- **Privacy**: Teach your child everyone has a right to privacy during bathing, dressing, and changing clothes. Knock on closed doors.

- **Bedrooms and bathrooms:** Most sexual abuse occurs in one or both. Set clear rules and guidelines regarding sharing bedrooms, being in another person's bed, being in the bathroom when someone else is there, and sharing bath times. Sexually abused children should have a "safe space" rather than sharing a bedroom. If separate bedrooms are not possible, consider using partitions to create separate spaces.

- **Touching:** Inform your child that no one should touch another person without permission. Tell her that private parts are to be touched only by a medical doctor during an examination **in your presence**. If your child is very young, explain that you may help with bathing or toileting.

- **Clothing on:** Family rules should include no nudity or walking around in underwear.

- **Setting limits and saying "no:"** Practice assertiveness with your child and how to say "no" clearly when someone touches them in an uncomfortable way.

- **Emergency plan**: Teach your child actions to take if someone goes beyond their limits after they say, "no." Teach about safety plans, whom to call, that it's okay to scream for help.

- **Sex education**: Teach your child basic sexual information such as correct names for body parts—penis, vagina, breasts, and buttocks. Explain what pornography is and what to do if they are exposed to it. Pornographic material should not be in your home.

- **Sexualized language:** Set a family rule that obscene or sexualized language is not allowed in your home.

- **Secrets**: Make sure you have a "no secrets" rule in your home. Tell your child to inform you immediately if someone asks them to keep a secret. Use the word "surprises," not "secrets" for special events.

- **Being alone with one person:** Protect your child. It's best not to leave your child alone with another adult. Be very selective and careful about where your child goes and with whom.

- **Wrestling and tickling** have sexual overtones. Do not allow these in your home. While they may seem normal, children often feel helpless, overpowered, or humiliated.
- Help your child understand the difference between **thoughts, feelings, and actions**. Discuss choice and responsibility.

Building your child's skills

Sexually abused children show predictable emotions, behavior and relationship patterns. These include withdrawal, mood swings, anger, self-harm, confusion, lack of concentration and focus, inability to listen to and follow instructions, unreasonable demands, avoidance, deliberately annoying other people, and blaming others for their mistakes or misbehavior. Your child's stress response is "on", and he does not know how to turn it "off." Being aware and prepared for these will help you keep your emotions separate and be more available to support your child.

Trauma has a profound effect on a child's physical and psychological development. Sexually abused children find it difficult to trust other people, feel safe, understand and manage emotions, adjust to change, and manage stress. Your child needs to learn skills, such as mindfulness, self-calming, self-soothing, stress management, emotion recognition and regulation, assertiveness, and other self-regulation skills. Learn how to parent your traumatized child! While your child's therapist will help your child with skills, you have an important opportunity to create a safe home environment for your child to learn and practice skills. Creating a structured, safe, and nurturing home is the best gift you can give your child. He or she can develop resilience, increase self-esteem, and overcome barriers to recovery.

You can increase your child's self-esteem by providing opportunities to excel in activities he enjoys. Sports, music programs, drama, dance, art, Boy or Girl Scouts and 4-H Clubs offer opportunities for achievement and success. Your consistent support of and presence in these activities also helps him feel valued and important. You can also encourage your child to increase her self-esteem by helping others through community service and volunteering.

As mothers of sexually abused children, we teach our children the world is safe, and they can feel confident, capable, and lovable. You help your child learn positive behaviors, thoughts and actions. You help your child build resilience, the ability to bounce back from trauma and thrive, by:

- Building strong, supportive relationships;
- Nurturing talents and abilities;
- Empowering them through choices and responsibilities;
- Connecting them with the larger community through activities.

Dr. Bruce Perry, U.S. child trauma psychiatrist, stated, "The healthier relationships a child has, the more likely he will be to recover from trauma and thrive. Relationships are the agents of change and the most powerful therapy is human love."[30]

Help your child become a survivor, not a victim. You assist him with respect for self and others, friends and positive relationships, and success in school and activities. In time, with support, therapy, and coping skills, he can move past the abuse. To encourage resilience and future happiness, you aim to quickly reverse negative core beliefs of being unworthy, unlovable, and unsafe. Let him know he is a survivor!

Parenting a Traumatized Child

Viewing your child's behaviors through a "trauma lens" helps you understand their behavior. Your child may feel physically safe, not psychologically safe. Aim to create an environment of both physical and psychological safety.

Your child may react to certain people, places or events reminding him or her of the abuse. Anything associated with the trauma can be a trigger, including sights, smells, tastes, sounds, sensations, people, places, colors, textures, words, emotions.

Remember: This is not a conscious process. Your child may be unaware of the connections and may react with extreme emotions. You may never know what triggered your child.

Neither of you can prevent these trigger moments. When your child is triggered, calmness, acceptance, patience and mindfulness work well. Notice, pay attention, be present and supportive. You may change your child's physical surroundings, especially if the abuse occurred in your home (for example, changing bedrooms, bedding, adding nightlights). Promote your child's sense of safety any way you can.

Posttraumatic stress disorder (PTSD) occurs when a trauma victim experiences hyperarousal, re-experiencing, withdrawal or avoidance. Many, though not all, children and moms, develop PTSD. You or your child may experience a few or numerous PTSD signs.

- **Hyperarousal** means your child is unable to calm himself, He is anxious, jumpy, quick to startle, can't concentrate, and has trouble sleeping.
- **Re-experiencing** the trauma includes bad dreams or nightmares, memories that keep coming to mind, feeling the trauma is happening again, feeling upset, or experiencing strong physical reactions.
- **Avoidance** of thoughts about the trauma, memories, or reminders leaves your child feeling numb, frozen, shut down, separated from normal life. He or she may pull away from friends and activities.
- **Dissociation** is blocking negative emotions and experiences, separating or postponing a thought or feeling that would normally occur. It is absenting from life, the opposite of mindfulness, sometimes called zoning or spacing out, *not there.*
- **Negative thoughts and beliefs** about themselves and others, based on the trauma experience. These include believing something is "wrong" with them, blaming themselves, feeling distant or different from others, and having difficulty experiencing positive feelings.

These symptoms result in learning and sleep difficulties, moodiness or anger, and acting younger than their age. Behaviors may cause your child guilt, shame, fear and confusion. *Your* understanding of the connection between your child's behaviors and the abuse is essential.

Sometimes an abused child will act out sexually with another child when you were unaware that he or she had been sexually abused. This is very complex and painful for you. You must continue to give love and support to and get essential counseling for each. A very small percentage of sexually abused children become offenders; many sex offenders were abused as children. Therapy in childhood and adolescence can prevent adult sexually abusive behaviors.

Planning Positive Times

You can help your child recover by spending extra time with him or her. You can help all siblings by arranging times for fun and special events. Do not lose yourself in grief or legal action. Make new positive memories including laughter and play:

- Play games together;
- Take a walk together daily;
- Make favorite meals together;
- Watch a favorite movie and eat popcorn;
- Make s'mores in the fireplace and have a campout in the living room;
- Go camping;
- Go to the zoo;
- Walk on the beach and collect shells;
- Adopt a dog or cat;
- Go to the pet store and buy a gerbil, fish or a bird;
- Read a long book out loud for several days so you can all look forward to the time together;
- Start new family rituals: hot chocolate for breakfast, pancakes for supper once a week, one new activity together each week;
- Buy art materials and create art together;
- Hang out together, talk, and laugh.

You are busy with appointments for your child's counseling, investigation and prosecution. Enlist friends' and family help in planning special activities with siblings so they feel included. Ask selected trustworthy friends and family to include your other children in some of their family's events. Avoid focusing solely on the needs of your child victim; be mindful of and actively involved with your other children.

Parenting Siblings

Attend to siblings. While you are concerned with your sexually abused child, siblings are secondary victims; sometimes they too are primary, undisclosed, victims. After sexual abuse disclosure, siblings experience serious loss and often do not receive coping assistance. Their living and school arrangements, friendships and family relationships may be affected. They may feel helpless, victimized, and stigmatized. Your understanding and support are essential.

Common sibling responses following a child's sexual abuse disclosure may include:

- Denial or unwillingness to believe the report;
- Minimizing the abuse;
- Loyalty and alignment with the abuser;
- Guilt for knowing and not telling; guilt for not knowing; guilt for not caring;
- Shame about the perpetrator, the victim, the family, and about you for not stopping it all;
- Relief that the secret is out in the open; relief that they were not abused;
- Anger, anxiety, confusion, and hurt;
- Ambivalence about the family, the abuse, the perpetrator, and you; a pendulum swing of love and hate, relief and anger.

Siblings' immediate needs include:

- Inclusion in conversation about the abuse. Children should be informed in language they can understand with minimal content to avoid further trauma. Siblings are less anxious when they know what is happening in their family.
- Information about the disclosure. Conversations should take place with siblings individually, and if more than one, as a group, as soon as possible after disclosure. Assure them you will protect them.
- Involvement in all family interventions.
- Did the sibling
  - ► Know about the abuse? If so, how did they find out—from the victim, perpetrator, or another person?
  - ► Witness the abuse?
  - ► How long has the sibling known about the abuse?
  - ► What prevented the sibling from reporting the abuse—fear, threats, or a promise to keep the secret?

- ‣ Was the sibling sexually abused by the same or another perpetrator?
- ‣ Does the sibling know about others who have been or are being abused?
- Receiving counseling if they disclose sexual abuse; this will result in additional reports, medical examinations, and investigations.

Siblings also need:

- To be accepted and treated with patience;
- Reassurance they are loved. Touching a shoulder, hugging or rocking a child reassures your child that you are still there for her;
- To know they matter and their needs are important;
- Counseling as soon as possible after their sibling's disclosure. When the perpetrator is a parent, grandparent, or close family member, siblings suffer loss of an important relationship and will grieve;
- Depending on the perpetrator's identity, the sibling may deny the abuse occurred and align with the perpetrator. Negotiate your support role very carefully; support the victim and acknowledge the sibling's emotional turmoil;
- Siblings may be angry at you. They may blame you, believing you knew and did not protect. Respond by listening, supporting, loving, and understanding your child's pain and fear, not by trying to defend yourself;
- Siblings may also feel angry at the victim for telling, resulting in family animosity and divisions;
- Siblings may have known and not told about the abuse. They may feel guilty and responsible. All children must be told the perpetrator alone is responsible for the abuse.

Siblings realize their family is being torn apart and the future is unknown. They are afraid. You are a peacemaker, helping the children without unnecessary harm to their relationships. When the perpetrator is a family member, siblings observed or experienced relationship problems among family members, competition among siblings, secret-keeping, perhaps jealousy for attention to the victim. They may have experienced threats, violence, living in a sexualized environment, or observed sexual acts. They may feel either guilt or gratitude that they were not the victim. They may feel different and distance themselves from the victim. They need help dealing with a chaotic home environment.

Reality Check: Supporting the victim and other children will be emotionally draining. *Expect* this and take care of yourself by getting support and counseling.

Parenting Your Child Who Has Disclosed Abuse as an Adult

While disclosure in adulthood may bring similar disruption to your life as disclosure by your minor child, you may mistakenly believe your adult child "can handle it." **No! Disclosure by an adult child is emotionally as distressing as when a minor child discloses.** Your adult child may be living independently and may be an adult chronologically. His or her need for your belief, support and emotional protection will be as strong as if he were under 18. He or she would be the one to bring any legal action. You will have the same issues about your living arrangements, betrayal by a spouse or partner, and your adult child's need for your belief, support and protection. In some ways, it may be even more difficult for you to separate from your partner or spouse in order to support your adult child emotionally. Do not accept the view that, "she's an adult now and can take care of herself; I have to take care of myself." It's true that your child is chronologically an adult. Emotionally, she is reliving the abuse experience and feels vulnerable and abandoned. Do not defend yourself. Listen to and acknowledge her feelings of rage, hurt and betrayal. Let her know how sorry you are that this happened and you did not protect her. Tell her you will be there for her now and support her emotionally (and perhaps financially) through this crisis. When the abuser is your partner or spouse, you will have to make a choice. This will be very difficult for you. Use the supports described in **Chapter 5** to pull you through.

Other Challenges Mothers Face

You may face additional issues and relationship dynamics requiring your most effective coping skills. These challenges include:

- **Mother blaming**: While research has shown that most mothers respond very effectively following their child's disclosure of sexual abuse,[31] for many years, mental health, social services and legal professionals have tended to blame mothers, assuming prior knowledge of sexual abuse, unwillingness to protect your child, denial, and perceived weakness or inadequacy.[32] Although today mothers are considered secondary victims,[33] many professionals continue to maintain the disproved view of a mother's blame or complicity in the abuse.[34]

- **Responsibility**: Sometimes professionals partially blame mothers for the sexual abuse, considering mothers co-responsible, complicit, or co-offenders because they did not know or protect. This reinforces mothers' guilt and self-blame. *Remember*: **All responsibility for the abuse belongs to the abuser**.

- **Betrayal bonds**: Child victims and mothers often are bound to their abusers by betrayal bonds. You may be caught in internal loyalty conflict, especially to a partner or spouse, versus standing up for your child. A combination of psychological, emotional, and physical factors may create traumatic bonds in victims. Stockholm Syndrome is an example of betrayal bonds in which the victim develops (or has) an emotional bond with the perpetrator that serves as a survival strategy for the victim.[35]

- **Learned helplessness**: Victims of domestic violence and physical, emotional and sexual abuse experience pervasive helplessness and feel powerless to prevent the recurrence of abuse.[36]

- **Codependency:** Caretaking or rescuing others and taking responsibility for the consequences of another's behaviors. Mothers are sometimes viewed as codependent with abusers. You may not want your partner to suffer the negative consequences of going to jail or prison. Most mothers, seek to protect their child and will report sexual abuse. You must focus on the abuser's responsibility, legal consequences for abusive behavior, and your responsibility to protect your child no matter who the abuser.

- **Your trauma history**: You may have experienced trauma previously in your life. Your experience of learning about and dealing with your child's sexual abuse may bring back memories of your other trauma and affect your ability to respond to the current crisis. Obtaining expert and trustworthy help for yourself is essential so that you can believe, support and protect your child in crisis now.

- **Your sexual abuse history:** If you experienced sexual abuse as a child, your child's disclosure may trigger painful memories, whether or not you reported your own abuse. You may experience flashbacks and nightmares. Therapy is essential to resolve your abuse memories as they relate to your child's recent abuse.

- *Remember:* Your experiences are not the same as your child's. Try to keep your memories separate from your thoughts about your child's abuse. **You are not responsible for the abuse you suffered then and you are not responsible for your child's abuse now.** Some moms believe they could have prevented and should have known about the abuse, and feel guilty that they were unable to protect their child. **Let go of the guilt. The abuser is 100% responsible.**

- **Financial issues:** Financial concerns add stress. You may be dealing with financial problems including court, attorney, and counselor fees. When your partner is the abuser and must leave the family, income may be radically reduced. You may have difficulty maintaining your home, car payments, and paying bills. You may have to arrange childcare so you can work outside your home.

- **Future relationships:** Whoever the abuser is, your trust in others will be negatively impacted; a *normal* trauma response results in feelings of decreased safety. If you later form a close relationship or remarry, your reduced trust may create difficulties with intimacy, sharing childcare responsibility and decision-making.

CHAPTER SUMMARY

This chapter discussed positive parenting as a MOSAC and skill-building for your child. **Chapter 7** will address how to protect your child from future abuse and assure and maintain your child's safety.

CHAPTER 7

Protect: How Do I Keep My Child Safe So This Won't Happen Again?

Overview

Once you and your children have experienced the horror of child abuse, you are understandably afraid that, despite your best efforts, it will happen again. You need information about effective strategies for ongoing protection.

When your child has been sexually abused, he or she is at high risk of being re-abused. Your active protection of and vigilance over your children are essential. You want your children to know how to avoid abuse and what to do if it happens. Counseling and skill development may prevent abuse or bring awareness so disclosure occurs more quickly. Trust your gut and stand your ground. If a person's words or actions set off your alarms, allow no contact with your child.

This chapter addresses:

- Individual and environmental protective and risk factors;
- Resilience;
- Talking with your child about sexual abuse;
- Alert list;
- Teaching self-protection;
- General rules and guidelines;
- Rules for home and family visits;
- When a sibling is the abuser;
- Internet guidelines;
- Emergency plan;

- Protecting when legal action does not move forward;
- Protecting your adult child.

Remember: Children are vulnerable. You are their first line of defense.

Individual and environmental protective factors

Children's internal protective abilities can be developed and strengthened. You can help your child learn new skills, attitudes, and behaviors at home that support her learning in counseling. With these skills, your child is at **lower risk** of sexual abuse:

- Effective coping;
- Emotional regulation;
- Positive self-esteem;
- Social interaction;
- Supportive friendships;
- Academic success;
- Ability to ask for help;
- Age-appropriate independence.

These family and community characteristics **may be protective**:

- Higher socioeconomic status;
- Employed parents;
- Safe housing;
- Family involvement in spiritual community;
- Safe educational options;
- Role models and community member mentors;
- Health care coverage.

Your home environment is **critical** to protection. The following help protect your child:

- Your child's secure attachment to you (parent/caregiver);
- Positive parental relationship;
- Emotionally stable parents who freely praise and provide positive feedback;
- Stable household with structure, predictable schedule, rules and expectations;

- Sense of personal safety;
- Parents/partners who provide effective limits and discipline; monitor and supervise your child, limiting where she goes, what homes he visits, and who provides supervision;
- Positive peer relationships;
- Positive connections with extended family members and other adults;
- Open family communication, including sexual abuse education (good touch, bad touch);
- You monitor computer use;
- You and your child develop and discuss a safety plan;
- You honor your instinct and intuition regarding extended family members, friends, and strangers.

Risk factors

Your child is at **higher risk** of sexual abuse as a result of:
- Younger age, disability, prior history of trauma and abuse;
- Child qualities such as being trusting, outgoing, obedient or assertive;
- Being loud or withdrawn, unhappy and depressed, disobedient;
- Poor self-esteem;
- Physical and mental health problems;
- Exposure to potential adult perpetrators;
- Unstable home environment and parental marital status;
- Unstable parental emotional status and prior abuse history;
- Unreliable supervision;
- Poor parental protection;
- Family isolation, lack of community involvement;
- Problematic family dynamics, poor communication; family code of secrecy.

Younger children are at greater risk because they are smaller and more powerless than older children or adults. They lack life knowledge to dispute abusers' statements, and are unable to defend themselves. Children depend on adults for knowledge and information and assume parents are more aware than they are. The myths of mother "having eyes in the back of her head" and "always knowing" suggest you *knew* about the abuse. If you do not act to protect your child, he may *assume* you knew and did not care. Making sure the child is never alone with an adult is a good practice.

Children's basic developmental need for adult touch, love and affection creates risks. As children do not inherently know the difference between appropriate or "good" and inappropriate or "bad" touch, you must teach them.

As described in **Chapter 3**, your child may not be able to disclose abuse. When family rules prevent your child from talking freely, he may not know how to say, "no," to an adult.

Risks **must** be decreased so your child lives in a safe, supportive family. These include:

- Treatment of parental substance abuse, domestic violence and mental health conditions;
- Counseling to increase parental coping and emotional regulation skills;
- Parenting classes to strengthen relationships with children;
- Structured household rules and expectations to increase safety;
- Improved relationships with extended family members to provide additional positive support;
- Positive, loving relationships between parents/partners to increase emotional safety and support.

Protective factors may offset some risk factors. For example, while you may be a single mother, supportive family members and friends may help, and you may be active in your community. Poverty alone is not a predictor; living in a neighborhood with high drug abuse and crime rates increases risk.

Remember: Healthy families are respectful with clear boundaries and expectations. Practicing, teaching, and reinforcing these qualities reduces risks.

Resilience

Resilience is the ability to adapt well when faced with sexual abuse or trauma or other adverse circumstances. Human beings can adapt to change, and, like a rubber band when stretched, can bounce back. It is possible to learn behaviors and develop resources that will help you and your child recover faster. Resilience increases through:

- Supportive, caring relationships;
- Role models who encourage and help;
- Self-knowledge, self-awareness, and self-insight;
- Positive self-esteem, believing in yourself;
- Positive self-efficacy, knowing you *can* do what you need to do;
- Ability to solve problems, make decisions, and follow through with plans;
- Feeling empowered and autonomous;
- Self-efficacy and optimism reinforced by external support;
- Emotional regulation skills;
- Stress management and positive coping skills;
- Communication and assertiveness skills;
- Empathy for others;
- Hope and optimism;
- Spirituality;
- Flexibility;
- Humor.

Teaching Your Child Resilience

Mothers can increase their children's resilience by focusing on assets and strengths, and helping children use supportive resources.

You can:

- **Demonstrate your unconditional love with words and affection**;
- Provide structure and consistency to promote safety;
- Be a role model;
- Praise your child frequently to increase self-esteem and self-worth;
- Encourage independence and autonomy;

- Help your child learn to identify and manage emotions;
- Involve your child in decision-making and explain your decisions;
- Encourage empathy and compassion for others;
- Assist your child in learning positive communication and assertiveness skills;
- Communicate with your child about daily events and feelings. Keep the door open so your child feels safe in discussing her concerns. **Communication with your child is essential**;
- Teach responsibility and the connection between behavior and consequences;
- Accept your child **no matter what**. Communicate acceptance so your child will accept both himself and others.

Talking with Your Child about Sexual Abuse

Discussing sexual abuse is as important as any other health or safety rule, such as looking both ways when crossing the street and being careful. We must clearly warn about unsafe people, whether strangers or family members. Be specific and detailed in teaching safety. Answer your child's questions directly. Be sure to ask, "Do you understand?" and "Did I answer your question?" Listen carefully.

Teach your children:

- Their bodies belong to them; no one may touch them without permission;
- It's okay to say "no" to any adult;
- Correct names for body parts, including breasts, buttocks, penis, vagina, anus, etc.
- The difference between good touch, like hugging; and bad touch, like hitting; and confusing touches that feel "funny," uncomfortable, scary, or embarrassing;
- What to do if someone touches their private parts or asks something "funny" or "odd," or accidentally-on-purpose touches them in a confusing way;
- To trust their own feelings about touch; even young children can tell when someone's touch, request, or behavior feels uncomfortable;

- To talk to a trusted adult if they are not sure something is okay;
- "Yell, Run, Tell" steps if/when someone touches them inappropriately or they feel uncomfortable, telling a trusted adult *immediately;*
- By playing "what if" games, making sure they understand. For example, "what if someone put his hand on your bottom?" or "What if someone followed you home from school?"
- By practicing yelling a response like, "No, I don't like that!"
- Who the trusted adults are in their lives; who is safe to tell;
- How to tell; language and confidence to tell a safe person;
- Bad secrets make you feel sad, unhappy, and scared; do not keep secrets;
- Telling about sexual abuse is never "tattling" on another person;
- *Always* tell, even if someone has bribed, threatened, or blackmailed them; you will protect them and keep them safe;
- It is okay **not to hug** someone or sit on their lap, even if a family member, if you are uncomfortable. This respects your child's feelings. Forcing hugs with or sitting on an adult's lap unwillingly predisposes to submitting to sexual abuse.

Remember: Children must believe they will be heard and believed by a trusted adult, or they won't tell. Children fear not being believed, getting in trouble, and their parents' anger. Reassure your child that sexual abuse is **never** her fault, and it is your job to protect her.

Alert List

Teach your child to be alert and what to do if he notices certain behaviors, whom to contact and how to communicate his concerns in *all* circumstances. Training and practice can help.

Teach your child to be *alert* and follow the "Yell, Run, Tell" rule, if an adult, older child, or teenager does one of the following:

- Treats you differently than he or she treats other children;
- Wants to spend time alone with you;
- Gives you special privileges or gifts so you feel you owe him something;

- Tells you not to tell your mother or others about things he is saying or doing;
- Asks you to do things to him or her that involve physical touch;
- Does things to you that involve physical touch;
- *Accidentally* touches your private parts when you feel it was on purpose;
- Comes into your room when you are undressing or in the bathroom;
- Comes into your bedroom when you are sleeping;
- Says sexual things to you about your body or clothing;
- Walks around with bathrobe open or wearing minimal clothing or nude;
- Wants to show you pornography to *teach you about sex;*
- Wants to show you his body or touch your body to *teach you about sex;*
- Talks about sexual things that they have done;
- Talks about private things that involve his wife or your mother;
- Treats you like an adult, while he acts like a kid;
- If you are a teenager, asks you what you are doing sexually with your girlfriend or boyfriend.

Teaching Self-Protection

Children often do not disclose sexual abuse because they do not know it is wrong. You must teach your children what abuse is and how to respond to an abuser. Children are also afraid when a perpetrator is coercive and threatening. Sex offenders are highly skilled in manipulation and grooming. Teaching self-protective strategies increases empowerment and overcomes helplessness, hopelessness and negative emotions.

Remember: Sexual abuse is **never** your child's responsibility.

Children need to learn and understand:

- Definition of all types of abuse, including sexual abuse;
- Explanation of good touch and bad touch;
- Definition of a secret and importance of not holding secrets;

- What a sex offender is;
- Why sex offenders abuse children;
- How to protect themselves from abuse;
- Whom and how to tell if they are uncomfortable or have been abused;
- What to do if someone they know is being abused;
- What happens after they tell about the abuse.

Major self-protection areas:

- **Safety:** Information about sexual abuse, recognition of unsafe people, feelings, and safety with strangers, community members, and family;
- **Body awareness:** Knowledge about their bodies, private parts, and how their bodies function;
- **Communication**: How to express emotions and set boundaries;
- **Sex education**: Accurate age-appropriate information about sexual development, behavior, and reproduction;
- **Touching:** Good and bad touch and privacy;
- **Secrets**: What secrets are and how to *tell* a secret when feeling unsafe;
- **Encouragement to tell and not hold secrets**: Know mothers want them to tell secrets and understand why telling secrets helps;
- **Healthy relationships**: Understand the difference between healthy and unhealthy relationships and how to know relationships are safe or unsafe;
- **Assertiveness**: Learn to say "no," how to use their *voice*, stand up for themselves, and make sure they are *heard*.
- **Self-defense**: How to fight back when it is safe to do so.

Rules and Guidelines

Children feel safer with clear rules and boundaries. A family Safety Plan defines expectations at home and in the community. Set aside time for your family to develop a Safety Plan with rules and guidelines.

General House Rules: while families differ, make sure you include rules regarding:

- **Clothing**: In all home common areas, appropriate clothing to be worn, including underwear or pajamas under robes;
- **Respect:** For all family members, zero tolerance for threats or intimidation;
- **Kindness Golden Rule**: Do to others what you want done to you.
- **Pornography**: **None** allowed at home.
- **Tickling/wrestling: Not allowed**. Sexual abuse often occurs during this type of play. Children can feel afraid, powerless, helpless, and have no sense of control.

Bedroom Rules

- **Bedrooms**: Siblings do not share bedrooms.
- If sibling abuser lives in your home, the **sibling abuser's bedroom door is alarmed** at night.
- **Individual beds**: Everyone has a bed and sleeps in it.
- **Younger children's bedrooms** are close to parents' room.
- **Knocking** must occur before entering room.
- **Night lights** are recommended for all children to increase sense of safety.
- **Doors are closed** when changing clothes, and doors are open when children are playing in bedroom.

Bathroom Rules

- **One person at a time**: No one else is in the bathroom when another person is there.
- Family members **do not bathe or shower together.**
- Family members are not present when others are using the **toilet.**

Entertainment Rules: Establish rules for use of computers, internet, television, telephone, movies, and electronic games.

- **Computers** are monitored, and activities supervised;
- **Internet** access restrictions and safety rules are given to children;
- **Television:** Approved program list, clear boundaries, parental supervision;

- **Telephones**: Parental monitoring; rules appropriate to child's age;
- **Movies**: Guidelines for viewing; supervision, and discussion of movies;
- **Electronic games**: Monitored use, rules regarding content; supervision.

Physical Contact Rules:

No

- Wrestling;
- Tickling;
- Playing doctor;
- Hugging unless permission requested first;
- Kissing unless child initiates; never ask a child to kiss *anyone;*
- **Touching ever** in private areas.

Parents' Bedroom Rules: Mother's or parents' room is off-limits to children. Unless invited into the room, the child is not there.

Secrets: Eliminate all secret-keeping.

Childcare at Home

The perpetrator:

- Never babysits children;
- Is never alone with younger children or developmentally delayed family members;
- Never changes a diaper or child's clothing;
- Is not present and does not assist when young child is bathed.

These rules, with potential consequences for violations, should be discussed as a family. All family members should sign a formal agreement, with each having their own signed copy. This formalizes rules and emphasizes their importance.

Rules when Sibling is Abuser

If another of your children is the abuser, you continue to be **responsible for both**. The abuser needs to be in ongoing therapy and may be at significant risk of self-harm. Your emotions will be even more complex as you address your children's very different needs. Your loyalty and emotional energy will be split, and your own guilt and self-blame will be intensified. While supporting both, you must protect one from the other. Professionals working with your child will consult with you about your child's readiness for return home. You will face space and supervision difficulties, including:

- Sleeping arrangements **must** minimize risk and provide a sense of safety to the victim and other children at home;
- Close supervision: Mothers **must** be close by, alert, and aware;
- Limits and restrictions regarding spaces where abuser is allowed;
- Bathroom use **must** have specific rules to insure privacy and protection;
- Family secrets **must** be prohibited;
- Open communication will facilitate conversations about difficult topics;
- Adequate childcare arrangements assure a responsible adult is available for all childcare. Siblings are not to provide childcare;
- **No** wrestling, tickling, hide-and-seek, playing house.

Rules for Home and Family Visits

When the offender does not live at home, visitation may be allowed with rules from treatment or supervision providers. If the offender has not been convicted and/or is no longer supervised or in treatment, you must maintain the children's safety. The following rules are helpful:

Rules for Home Visits

- Cameras are installed in home;
- Offender is:
  - Always supervised;
  - **Never**
    - Enters a child's bedroom;
    - Oversees children's activities or disciplines a child;

- Sits next to a child or has child on lap;
- Involved in a child's physical hygiene;
- Engages in any type of play involving touching child;
- Family members lock doors after entering bathroom.

Remember: Sex offenders lack internal barriers to abusive behavior and rarely stop with only one victim. Sexual abuse becomes a habitual, situational pattern. *Protect all children in your home*, not just your child who disclosed sexual abuse.

Remember: Most sexual abuse victims do **not** report abuse when it occurs and may delay disclosure for months, years, or never tell. Offenders are highly skilled at normalizing sexual abuse. Children may have apparently normal and healthy relationships with the abuser, and if the abuse did not cause discomfort or pain, may not currently show symptoms. **Never** assume you "know" who has been abused. What your child has **not** told you, you do not know. **All** children are at risk with an abuser at home.

Rules for Overnight Visits

- All bedroom doors **must** have locks;
- Offender is **always**
  - Fully clothed;
  - Supervised;
- If awake at night, even for bathroom, offender **must** wake spouse or partner;
- Offender is **never** left alone with children;
- Offender **must** leave the home if children invite friends to spend the night.

Rules for Family Visits Outside the Home

- Offender is
  - **Always** supervised;
  - **Never** discusses the abuse with children;
  - **Never** around children's friends;
  - **Never** to have secrets with children;
  - **Never** to give gifts to children.

- Offender **never** disciplines children.
- Offender has **no physical contact** with children.
- Offender **never** sits next to children.

Internet Guidelines for Children

Parents must be responsible for and minimize potential risks of children's Internet use.

- Supervise your child's use of the computer with posted schedules, rules, and guidelines;
- Be familiar with technology and know all the sites your child visits;
- Make sure all devices have good filters, and monitor all online activities;
- Be aware of sexting and sexual communication among adolescents; discuss online risks;
- Keep children's computers in a family room with screen visible;
- Make sure you know your child's online friends as you know their other friends;
- **Never** allow your child to meet in person with someone met online;
- Do not allow your child to use computer excessively or late at night;
- Computers are not electronic babysitters;
- Inform service provider if child receives a harassing or sexual message;
- If transmission, use, or viewing or child pornography occurs, immediately report to CyberTipLine online or call 800-843-5678.

Children must know:

- **Never**
  - ▸ Share identifying information, such as address, phone, school or passwords;
  - ▸ Send their picture to anyone online;
  - ▸ Respond to suggestive, obscene, threatening, or uncomfortable online messages, and to tell you if this occurs;

114

- Some people on chat pages or games intend to hurt children;
- A person who identifies as a child or teenager may be lying;
- What your child sees online may be untrue.

Emergency Plan

Although you hope and plan for healing and recovery, prepare a detailed Emergency Plan in case you or your child are at risk and must act quickly. Information includes:

- **Identification**: Full name, date of birth, name of parent, address, phone number, and another safe person's name and phone number;
- **Telephone use**: How to use the phone, how to call you or another safe person, how to call 911;
- **Abuse response rehearsal**: What to do, whom to tell, how to tell;
- **Rehearse with your child whom to tell when in danger**: "If _____ happens, I will tell _____."
- **Develop a code**, one word your child uses if he feels unsafe, afraid, or someone has done something to him, to let you know something has happened;
- **Plan for your child to deal with all abuse situations**, including perpetrators who are strangers, community members, and family members;
- **Teach your child never to open the door to strangers**, to leave the house if the abuser is in your home, and possible escape routes from your home;
- **Help your child develop a "safety mind,"** paying attention to safety around him or her when in public, shopping, in the neighborhood, at home;
- **Make a list of safe places**, such as a place to use the phone or a place to stay;
- **Create a list of phone numbers to teach your child**, including names of family members, police, pastor or priest, neighbor, babysitter, parent's employer;
- **When in public with your child**, always keep him or her in sight;

- **Teach your child about strangers** and practice safety scenarios;
- **Teach your child to ignore adults who ask for directions** or try to start a conversation;
- **Teach your child it is okay to run away and scream** if necessary; where to go and whom to tell;
- **Never leave your child alone in a car** or unattended in a public place;
- **Teach your child what to do if separated from you** in a public place;
- **If your child has been sexually abused, and the perpetrator is living in the home again:**
  - ▸ Know your child's warning signs;
  - ▸ Know perpetrator's warning signs;
  - ▸ Have a plan of where to go, whom to call, what to do if you suspect abuse is re-occurring in your home.

Protecting Your Child When Your Case Isn't Confirmed

Though your child disclosed that her father abused her, perhaps the investigation did not confirm the allegation. As discussed in **Chapter 4**, many child sexual abuse cases lack enough evidence to proceed in court. If the abuser denies the allegation, and conviction has not occurred, your only recourse is to protect your child to the best of your ability in what seems like an impossible situation. The father has legal rights and the court will grant him access to your child. Your child is at **high risk** of continued sexual abuse.

You are your child's protector. The best protection is not having an abuser in your home. If married to or partnered with the abuser, do not reconcile. Do not reunify your family. While DHS will push for reunification, this is not in your child's best interests. Your child's safety is your primary concern. Do **not** believe an offender who says he is cured, or will never do it again, or did it because he was sick, impaired by alcohol, or asleep.

However, *if* you choose to have the abuser in your home, the safety rules and guidelines above will help you protect your child.

While separation and divorce only partially protect your child, they can increase safety. When you file for primary custody, his father can counter-file. Legal battles become *ugly*; an abuser will attack and lie in order to maintain access to your child. You cannot interfere with a father's visitation rights without facing potential legal consequences, including loss of custody.

Though you want to protect your child and deny the offender access, *you cannot do so!* The potential outcome may risk your child's safety even more. Your child needs to know you believe and support her and will do your best to protect her from ever being abused again. Yet you cannot promise this. Open communication and her ongoing therapy are essential. A mental health professional, who can testify in court, is the best protection you can provide. Try to arrange appointments soon after each visit with the abuser. Your child needs to be in therapy as long as the abuser has visitation, preferably within a day after each visit. Therapists are mandated reporters. Encourage your child to speak openly with his or her therapist. Therapists' recommendations, based on the child's welfare and best interests, are often accepted by the court. Professional support can also assist you in difficult decisions.

You are **not** helpless, nor is the situation hopeless! Keep a log of interactions with and behaviors of the abuser. Maintain a log of your child's concerning statements; prior to counseling appointments, inform his therapist. If your child discloses again, report immediately. With additional reports, the abuser may be arrested and charged. Your best legal recourse is to hire a very experienced attorney specializing in child sexual abuse, and keep fighting for the safety of your child.

You hope for justice for your child resulting in the abuser's arrest, conviction, and restricted access to children. Insist on supervised visits and oppose unsupervised visits with your child. Unsupervised visits are frightening for your child and nightmares for you, causing emotional upheaval and anxiety. You will suffer, **and** you can get help!

Remember: Your child needs a healthy parent to support her. You may have to *force* yourself to reach out for support. You must manage negative, fearful, angry feelings and create a safe home for your child.

When your abused child disclosed as an adult

You may mistakenly think you are off the hook about protection in this circumstance. However, your adult child will feel unsafe with *you* if you remain partnered with the abuser. She will perceive your separation from the abuser as a sign of your belief that she was abused along with your desire and willingness to support and protect her emotionally. If you stay with her abuser, she will feel unsupported, exposed and unprotected. She may become and remain estranged from you indefinitely. The cascade of emotions experienced by sexually abused children can be overwhelming in adulthood.

Remember: Your abused child may interpret the abuser's continued presence as betrayal by you. This perception will damage your relationship and may be a lifelong relationship barrier.

Remember: Denial and ambivalence may interfere with your ability to think clearly and make effective decisions. Maintain ongoing therapy and support.

CHAPTER SUMMARY

This chapter has addressed protection for your minor child, including when the abuser remains in your home or is a sibling. We discussed rules, guidelines, safety and emergency plans as well as the worst-case scenario in which the abuser has continuing access to your child.

Chapter 8 explores healing and recovery.

PART III

THERE IS LIFE AFTER SEXUAL ABUSE

Despite extreme psychological and physical injury, human beings are remarkably resilient, especially when safety and support enable healing and recovery.

This last section looks forward. You and your child will always bear scars from the injuries of child sexual abuse. However, with belief, protection and support, together with strengthened resilience, healing, recovery and a good life are possible.

CHAPTER 8

Healing and Recovery: Where Do I Go from Here?

Overview

We offer tools and skills for nurturing yourself, mothering your child, and going forward with your life while also supporting your child's growth into adulthood.

Mothers, how can you think about new beginnings? Can you start over after your child's sexual abuse? You and your child have both experienced trauma and possibly PTSD. Yet you and your child can learn, grow, and move forward. How?

Daily stresses and necessary legal action will affect you. Ongoing stress may result in poor physical health and illness, slowing healing and recovery. Be patient. Take care of yourself now, recognizing this journey will be long.

You may feel isolated. Friends and family are often conflicted. You live with secrets, stress and anxiety. Ask yourself why and for whose benefit you hold secrets.

You will learn a great deal as you recover. Therapy, support groups, and journaling all support personal growth and self-awareness. You can improve your emotional, physical, and mental health by using coping strategies to counteract stress. **Positive coping skills and a strong support system are the two most important elements promoting your recovery**. These include breathing, meditation, exercise, good nutrition, recreation, fun and social life. Choose activities to help you relax and increase enjoyment. These promote healing and recovery.

You can choose to be a survivor and a "thriver," rather than a victim of your child's sexual abuse. Although you may feel lowered self-esteem, guilt, responsibility, betrayal, and mental health difficulties, you can actively work to address these in your recovery. You can change the way you view yourself, your self-talk, resilience, and healthy boundaries. You can *choose* to grow and move forward in your life. You are not the victim you were. You can become a better mother and woman after what you have endured. Maintaining a positive attitude, not giving in to depression and despair, holding onto hope, and seeing a light at the end of the tunnel will help you in your recovery and growth.

- Commit to your own healing.
- Do not give up on yourself. While the road may be hard, you can travel it. Others have. You need to heal for yourself, for your abused child who needs your support, and for other children and family members who depend on you.
- Begin to trust yourself again. Be mindful of your thoughts, feelings, and perceptions.
- Be honest about your emotions, both to yourself and others. Be assertive, as necessary. Speak your truth.
- Although staying busy helps you cope with stress, do not get *too* busy. Allow yourself down-time for relaxing and enjoyable activities.
- Do not hide. It is easy to isolate and avoid. Reach out to others. Ask for help. Make new friends.
- Avoid unhealthy coping such as overuse of alcohol, drugs, and other addictive substances.
- Do not harm yourself. Do not overeat, begin or resume an eating disorder.
- If you are in trouble or thinking of hurting yourself, **ask for help**!

You can heal one day at a time. Each day is a new beginning. Each moment is an opportunity to be present and aware.

Truth and Denial

Acceptance of Reality and Truth

Yours and your child's recovery require you to be truthful with yourself about what happened and what's next. These truths are about *what is*, not what you want or hoped or thought. "*What is, is*" is a useful phrase. The period means that's the end of the statement.

Telling the truth means facing the good, the bad, and the ugly, including your thoughts, feelings, and beliefs, those of your child and others.

Rigorous honesty with ourselves means we remain in reality. We stay in the present; we are awake and aware of the present moment. *Mindfulness* is the opposite of dissociation. It is easy to dissociate, to put all the pain outside your conscious awareness so you don't have to think about it. When dissociated, you are not able to care for yourself or your child.

Telling yourself the truth is about *accepting* truth, moving out of denial into reality. This reduces stress, because we stop fighting. Though the circumstances do not change, our internal conflict is reduced. This is our new reality. Our child was abused. We were unable to prevent it. Now we move forward to support and protect our child, to make right choices and decisions. Simply "Doing the Next Right Thing" is a helpful mantra. While you cannot change reality, you can handle each problem to the best of your ability. Mindfulness increases your ability to feel your feelings, be aware of your thoughts, and accept the current reality of your life.

Telling yourself the truth does not mean telling everyone the truth. Choose those you can trust. This is self-care and boundary-setting. You do not have to say any of your thoughts or feelings out loud to anyone, unless you choose to do so with a trusted counselor, friend or family member. Some of these feelings are extraordinarily private. Protect yourself.

Denial of Reality and Truth

Denial is unhealthy coping, the opposite of accepting and facing reality. We escape reality by denying the event, its seriousness, our responsibility, and the consequences. Denial harms children's and mothers' best interests.

Continued denial prevents you from making protective, healthy decisions for your child. Avoid unhealthy coping, such as:

- **Acting out**: Avoiding reality through alcohol, drugs, gambling, overeating, cutting/self-harm, compulsive shopping, relationship/sexual impulsivity;
- **Help-rejecting complaining**: Asking for help, while hiding feelings and rejecting offers of help;
- **Intellectualizing**: Staying in intellectual understanding of events, while avoiding feelings;
- **Passive-aggression**: Being indirectly aggressive, rather than directly expressing anger and painful emotions; appearing compliant and agreeable, with resistance and hostility underneath;
- **Rationalizing**: Creating superficial logical justifications for impulsive and emotional actions and behaviors;
- **Minimizing**: Making little of an event, experience, or statement;
- **Escapism**: Using fantasy, books, movies, computer games, internet to escape real-life problems or avoid dealing with difficult emotions; remaining in an imaginary world, rather than the *real world*;
- **Splitting**: Dealing with emotional stressors by compartmentalizing negative and positive, not integrating the two for a *reality picture*, and dealing with ambivalence by going back and forth without resolution;
- **Repression**: Preventing distressing thoughts, feelings, and experiences from entering conscious awareness by pushing them down into the unconscious. Many sexual abuse victims repress large chunks of their childhood.

Fighting reality is like hitting your head against a wall. While the wall will not move, your head will hurt! In facing and recognizing the wall is there, you are mindful of its reality. Your fears of or anger at the wall are just feelings. Mindfulness is awareness without judgment. You accept life, yourself, others, situations, experiences as they are. This does not mean you approve, condone, agree, or like the situation or person; it means you face the reality, the essential "isness" of the situation.

You are here. What is *here* now? This is mindfulness. If you're brushing your daughter's hair and thinking about what happened to her or about her abuser and how horrible this is, or about the investigation, you will not experience the joy of brushing your daughter's hair, feeling its texture, or talking to her and listening, smelling the shampoo in her hair, seeing the shine, noticing the sun coming through the window, feeling the pleasure of this *one simple moment.* You would have lost all that.

Health Effects of Denial

When denial becomes a *habit of avoiding the truth,* it can result in increased health problems and lowered immune system function, making us vulnerable to illness. Dissociation leads to psychological distress appearing as physical illness. We experience stress in the body, rather than our emotions. Focusing on physical symptoms can reinforce inability to recognize, manage, and express emotions. Increased physical complaints and illnesses are *very* common among mothers of sexually abused children.[37]

Dissociation and physical illness negatively affect a mother's ability to support her child. Mothers of sexually abused children need both psychological and medical help, because her child's sexual abuse affects a mother in the deepest core of her being, impacting brain, emotions, body, and immune system. "Simply imagining what has happened to her child may flood a mother with horror or other symptoms consistent with posttraumatic stress disorder."[38]

Ongoing Pain and Hurt

Following disclosure and your child's initial recovery and adjustment, you may believe the worst consequences of the abuse have passed. This may be so. Some resilient victims, with support and good coping skills, may move beyond the post-disclosure phase without being negatively affected for the remainder of their lives. Most sexual abuse victims experience long-term consequences.

Support is essential for all mothers. We must fully understand we did not cause the abuse: the abuser is responsible. We must move through and beyond our initial emotional reactions. You will probably experience long-term consequences from your child's sexual abuse. This does not mean healing is not possible. However, our minds do not have a "delete" button. We will never forget what happened to our child, nor do we want to. We will continue to feel pain, even after the crisis is long past. In addition, you may also feel grief, betrayal and loss about the abuser, especially when a partner, husband, other family member, or friend.

Pain and hurt resurface even years afterward, as you observe your previously abused child struggling with adult relationships, continuing to have PTSD symptoms, or addicted to alcohol or other drugs. Years later, you may recognize unhealed aspects of your own life and effects on your current roles and relationships. Pay attention to your feelings and honor your ongoing pain and hurt. Though the pain will lessen over time, an acute ache may linger for many years.

Transforming Negative to Positive Thoughts and Feelings

After a child discloses sexual abuse, we struggle with intruding thoughts and obsess over the horror of the details. Negative thoughts affect our mood and reduce our ability to manage responsibilities as a mom, care for ourselves and maintain our health. Negative thoughts set off hormonal reactions that affect our immune system and overall health. Common intrusive, repetitive thoughts include denial, guilt and shame, anger, fear and helplessness.

Continuing to think these thoughts results in increased negativity, confusion, and ambivalence. You may get stuck here and get increasingly depressed, tired, and unable to cope. Learn to overcome these thoughts and shift your mind from negative to positive. We will experience pain, grief, and strong emotions. We *must* know how to manage these so we can move forward.

We can counter these thoughts with acceptance, mindfulness, positive self-talk, optimism, and empowerment.

- **Acceptance** is both an end-point and a process. You accept both the fact of the sexual abuse and the consequences for your child and yourself, and you have hope for the future.
- **Mindfulness** is being present in the here and now. It is feeling the feelings and sitting still with the thought without trying to push it away or avoid it. Mindfulness is being awake and aware about your life, moment by moment, accepting the "what is," the reality of your life.

- **Positive self-talk**: This dialogue affects your behaviors, choices, relationships, and self-esteem. You can think about what you're thinking. You can pay attention and catch negative thought patterns. Purposeful self-talk will increase your self-esteem. Use it to challenge your thoughts, rather than accepting them as fact. Positive self-talk will reduce your stress.
- **Learning optimism** is the opposite of learned helplessness. An optimist looks at conditions as temporary, while a pessimist looks at them as permanent. The optimist is convinced that circumstances will improve. A pessimist is convinced that negativity is permanent, the opposite of hopefulness. Positive self-statements will keep you moving forward in recovery, instead of getting stuck in hopelessness.
  - ‣ This too will pass.
  - ‣ It won't last forever.
  - ‣ I can get through this.
  - ‣ I can survive.
  - ‣ My child will recover.
- **Empowerment** means you choose, decide and are in charge of your life. You do *not* have control over other people, CPS, court systems; you *do* have control over yourself. Tell yourself, "I can," then act.
- **Self-efficacy** is the belief that you are can manage your life and reach your goals. Remain open to growth and change. Believe in yourself and move forward, both for yourself and your child.

After your child discloses sexual abuse, you struggle with severe stress including horrific negative thoughts. As you move into recovery, reconstructing your life with hope and revitalization, even if still managing legal and related problems, you *must* adopt more positive thought patterns.

Anger and Hatred

Anger, a normal first response, can fester for years. Acceptance of our anger is the first step. Then, we look at the emotions under the anger—hurt, fear, disappointment, worry, grief, betrayal—to determine what is driving the anger. We must then let it go. Anger's biological function is to alert us that something is wrong. Rather than continuing the anger, we then must *address what is wrong*.

Fear and Anxiety

Feelings of fear and anxiety are common during a chaotic, painful time. Be mindful about your emotions, be aware of feelings and know how to manage them. You can become anxious when something reminds you of the sexual abuse. Use anxiety-reducing skills to minimize fear and anxiety. Use previously described positive coping skills, other coping strategies from the MOSAC website, and those suggested by your counselor. If anxiety worsens and develops into panic attacks, see your physician and take care of yourself.

Choice, Problem-Solving, and Decision-Making

Choice

Choice requires using thoughts, feelings and intuition to identify the right thing is to do. You always have options, even if only the option to choose your attitude in an uncontrollable situation.

Carefully thought-through choices are the opposite of impulsive emotion-driven choices. Keys to effective choices are:

- Taking the time needed;
- Having a quiet mind and a relaxed body;
- Separating yours and others' responsibilities;
- Separating wants, needs, and obligations;
- Carefully weighing all options;
- Making the most effective choice, even if it involves loss or discomfort.

Mindfulness helps make choices clearer, as do truthfulness and reality-checking. Once you realistically see the choices before you, assertiveness is key. Stand up for your child and for yourself in very difficult situations on your recovery path. Make choices over which you have control regarding your child and yourself. Make the best choice given the circumstances.

Taking responsibility for choices is empowering. You can choose to survive and learn from this crisis, rebuild your life, and live a longer and happier life.

Problem-Solving

Resolving problems thoughtfully helps you feel more in control and less a victim.

- Your attitude affects the quality of your problem solution. A positive attitude is likely to lead to positive problem resolution.
- If you have faced this problem before, try thinking outside the box this time.

Everyone reacts differently. Since some reactions may be *automatic*, it is important to:

- Slow down;
- Define the problem and describe it clearly to yourself and others;
- Collect all the facts so you know the reality of the situation;
- Identify whether your beliefs are based on assumptions or facts;
- Elicit help and information from all available resources;
- Generate alternatives and evaluate anticipated consequences of each;
- Include thinking, feeling and intuition in the mix;
- After considered thought, come to your own conclusion regarding the solution;
- Determine the best possible *long-term* solution to the problem.

Decision-Making

You will face many decisions, some of which will be large, comprehensive, and life-altering. Early decisions involve reporting, protection and support for your child. Some decisions may be very, very difficult, confusing and ambivalence-causing, such as decisions about separation or divorce, staying or moving, finances, employment, and counseling. Use your journal to help with awareness of your fears. Know yourself, your values, and priorities. Sometimes you can only select from available alternatives. Other times, you may be able to identify new, creative alternatives by thinking "out of the box." The outcome of the decision is out of your hands. You do not control what happens next. Follow through by taking the next step. Practice acceptance of the outcome, use your coping skills, and maintain your stability in this time of change.

Future Relationships

You may find it difficult to trust yourself and others. A new relationship may provoke triggers. You may have posttraumatic symptoms, such as anxiety and hypervigilance. Your feelings of betrayal can interfere with future intimate relationships. Your coping skills and personal history influence your ability to trust.

Prior to engaging in a new relationship, you can benefit from counseling. You and a potential new partner may benefit from couples counseling to increase your new partner's awareness of family dynamics and areas of risk. The prior abuse, post-trauma triggers, and potential effects on the new relationship must be discussed. You can then plan to manage difficult times together.

Some areas to consider in a new relationship include:

• Sexual intimacy;
• Partner's behavior and communication with your child;
• Your child's possible rejection of the new partner because of trust issues;
• Bath and shower times;
• Bedtimes and early mornings;
• Leaving the partner alone with your child;
• Sharing childcare.

Without explicit discussion, your new partner may assume an unrealistic "normalcy." Open communication and planning are essential. Introducing a new partner to your child, followed by subsequent departure of this partner from the family, would be another trauma for your child. Be careful, go slowly, and communicate well.

Financial Issues

Financial issues may add stress. Additional expenses and reductions in family income may result from attorney's and counseling fees, childcare and transportation expenses.

When the offender was your family's primary wage earner, financial consequences *may* include loss of family home, change of children's schools, inability to maintain car payments, and application for food stamps or other state assistance. If you have been working outside your home, you may not be able to maintain your work schedule while meeting legal, investigative, therapeutic, and court appointments. Your emotions may also interfere with your work performance. Financial considerations can unconsciously affect your feelings about possible reunification.

Discuss finances and relief options with your counselor and knowledgeable advisors, and access available assistance. Financial assistance for victims, including mothers, is often available at the courthouse through Victim Advocacy offices. Face what is most important—your child's safety—and plan a financial strategy that assures safety and rebuilds your financial life.

Remember: Your role is to believe, protect, and support your child. The choices, problem-solving, and decisions we make **must** best protect and support our abused child. Always consider your child's best interests **first**. We nevertheless must be as consciously aware as possible of our needs and wants, even if we must delay accomplishing some of our personal goals in order to nourish our children. Maintaining and supporting our own well-being is essential for our health and personal growth as well as that of our children.

Anticipatory Coping

Being aware of some of the challenges you will face on your recovery journey can help you manage them more effectively. While your focus now is on healing and recovery, learning and practicing skills to deal with trigger moments and difficult decisions will increase your ability to deal with unexpected "curveballs." Painful memories, especially when unexpected, can take us right back to trauma. When triggered, it's helpful to remind ourselves "it's not happening now."

Recognizing there will be difficult times and practicing in advance can help us feel more capable and competent when those moments do occur. We can tell ourselves, "yes, I recognize this; I'm having a flashback;" or "I feel as if the crisis is happening all over again." Then we can use mindfulness, self-talk and other skills to remind ourselves we've come a long way. Though this moment may be upsetting, the original crisis and trauma are **not** repeating now. We can be resilient, adapt, acknowledge the pain and move on. We and our children are no longer victims; we are survivors and thrivers. Your child's recovery **and** your recovery are both important and possible. There is healing, recovery and life after child sexual abuse.

CHAPTER SUMMARY

This chapter has explored some of the challenges of your recovery path. There **is** life after sexual abuse. You and your child will always carry scars from these wounds, though as has been said, we can use these to make ourselves stronger and more resilient; we do not have to keep re-opening the wounds. There will be times, often unexpected, when we feel ambushed by triggers that bring us back to our wounded places. With the positive skills we have learned, we can acknowledge those painful times and their scars, remembering "it is **not happening now.**" Then we can be kind and caring to ourselves, withdraw as necessary to tend to our old wounds, and re-emerge ready to live fully. Though we never fully forget, we can move forward as survivors, thrivers and *former* victims. Setting this example can also help our previously abused child acknowledge and recover from other life wounds.

The goal of this **Guide** has been to give you information, understanding and support to help you through this very difficult experience, while believing, supporting and protecting your child and nourishing yourself as well towards a rewarding and fulfilling new life. We hope as a result, you will be better off than those of us who had little information and minimal understanding and support when our lives were upended by our child's sexual abuse.

We believe knowledge is power. The better we understand child sexual abuse, the more we can provide the essential support our children need and deserve; and the more likely we and they are to emerge as survivors and thrivers rather than as lifelong victims.

We encourage you to explore the resources in the **Appendix** including online sources and the MOSAC Mothers' Facebook Group.

Thank you for joining us on this journey,
Mel Langston, Leona Puma and recovering mothers

CHAPTER NOTES

Chapter 1

1. The Leadership Council on Child Abuse & Interpersonal Violence (2005), "How often do children's reports of abuse turn out to be false?" Retrieved from www.leadershipcouncil.org/1/res/csa-acc.html February 12, 2019.

Chapter 2

2. www.Victimsofcrime.org/media/reporting-on-child-sexual-abuse/statistics-ion-perpetrators-of-csa, retrieved February 19, 2019.

3. United States Department of Health and Human Services, Administration for Children and Families, Administration on Children, Youth and Families, Children's Bureau, Child Maltreatment Survey, 2016 (2018).

4. https://www.rainn.org/statistics/scope-problem

5. Briere, J., & Eliot, D.M. (2003). Prevalence and psychological sequence of self-reported childhood physical and sexual abuse in general population, *Child Abuse & Neglect, 27,* 10; Centers for Disease Control and Prevention, Kaiser Permanente (2016). The ACE Study Survey Data (Unpublished Data). Atlanta, GA: U.S. Department of Health and Human Services.

6. www.Rainn.org/statistics/children-and-teens; U.S. Department of Health and Human Services, Administration for Children and Families, Administration on Children, Youth and Families, Children's Bureau, Child Maltreatment Survey, 2016 (2018).

7. Black, M.C., et al. (2011). The National Intimate Partner and Sexual Violence Survey (NISVS): 2010 Summary Report. Atlanta, GA: National Center for Injury Prevention and Control, Centers for Disease Control and Prevention https://www.cdc.gov/violenceprevention/pdf/nisvs _report201-a.pdf

8. Smith, D., et al. (2000). Delay in disclosure of childhood rape: Results from a national survey. *Child Abuse & Neglect, 24,* 273–287; Broman-Fulks, J.J., et al. (2007). Sexual assault disclosure in relation to adolescent mental health: Results from the National Survey of Adolescents. *Journal of Clinical Child and Adolescent Psychology, 36(2, April),* 260–266.

9. www.rainn.org/statistics/children-and-teens; U.S. Department of Health and Human Services, Administration for Children and Families, Administration on Children, Youth and Families, Children's Bureau, Child Maltreatment Survey, 2016 (2018).

10. Miller, K.L., Dove, M.K., & Miller, S.M. (2007, October). A counselor's guide to child sexual abuse: Prevention, reporting and treatment strategies. Paper based on a program presented at the Association for Counselor Education and Supervision Conference, Columbus, OH: National Association of Adult Survivors of Child Abuse (NAASCA) (2012). http://www.naasca.org/2012-Resources/010812 -StatisticsOfChildAbuse.htm, retrieved January 14, 2019.

11. Centers for Disease Control and Prevention, Kaiser Permanente (2016). The ACE Study Survey Data (Unpublished Data). Atlanta, GA: U.S. Department of Health and Human Services.

12. Finkelhor, D., Crimes Against Children Research Center. https://www .victimsofcrime.org/media/reprting-on-child-sexual-abuse/child-sexual -abuse-statistics

13. www.mosac.net/page/190, retrieved February 19, 2019.

14. www.victimsofcrime.org/media/reporting-on-child-sexual-abuse/child -sexual-abuse-statistics, retrieved February 19, 2019.

15. www.rainn.org/statistics/children-and-teens; U.S. Department of Health and Human Services, Administration for Children and Families, Administration on Children, Youth and Families, Children's Bureau, Child Maltreatment Survey, 2016 (2018).

16. Greenfeld, L. (1997, February). Sex Offenses and Offenders. An analysis of data on rape and sexual assault. U.S. Department of Justice, Office of Justice Programs, Bureau of Justice Statistics. Retrieved from https://bjs .gov/content/pub/df/SOO.PDF

17. Greenfeld, L. (1997, February). Sex Offenses and Offenders. An analysis of data on rape and sexual assault. U.S. Department of Justice, Office of Justice Programs, Bureau of Justice Statistics. Retrieved from https://bjs .gov/content/pub/df/SOO.PDF

18. https://www.cnn.com/2018/01/24/us/rachael-denhollander-full -statement/index.html

19. https://www.cdc.gov/violenceprevention/childabuseandneglect/acestudy/ index.html

20. Perry, B. D., & Szalavitz, M. (2007). *The boy who was raised as a dog: And other stories from a child psychiatrist's notebook: what traumatized children can teach us about loss, love and healing.* Basic Books.

Chapter 3

21. London, K., Bruck, M., Ceci, S., & Shuman, D. (2003) Disclosure of child sexual abuse: What does the research tell us about the ways that children tell? *Psychology, Public Policy, and Law, 11*(1), 194–226; Ullman, S. E. (2007). Relationship to perpetrator, disclosure, social reactions, and PTSD symptoms in child sexual abuse survivors. *Journal of Child Sexual Abuse, 16*(1), 19–36.

22. Knott, T., & Fabre, A. (2014). Maternal response to the disclosure of child sexual abuse: Systematic review and critical analysis of the literature. *IPT Journal-Forensics, 20:* 1–7.

23. Everson, M., & Boat, B. (1989). False allegations of sexual abuse by children and adolescents. *Journal of the American Academy of Child and Adolescent Psychiatry 28* (2): 230–235.

24. This is my experience in 30 years as a clinician seeing children who have been sexually abused, their mothers and abusers. When abusers are charged with a crime, some do admit their crime. One study found that confession was more likely when suspects were younger and more evidence of abuse was available, especially child disclosure and corroborating evidence. This suggests that supporting child disclosure and obtaining confirming evidence increases the likelihood of confession of accused suspects. See Lippert, T., Cross, T.P., Jones, L., & Walsh, W. (2010). Suspect confession of child sexual abuse to investigators. *Child Maltreatment, 15* (May, 2), 161–70. https://doi.org/10.1177/1077559509360251

25. Forrest, S. (2017) Study: Supreme Court decision complicates prosecuting child abusers. *Illinois News Bureau,* July 19. https://news.illinois .edu/view/6367/532785#:~:text=Nearly%2042%20percent%20of%20the ,greatly%E2%80%9D%20or%20%E2%80%9Csomewhat.%E2%80%9D

Chapter 4

26. Under normal circumstances, mothers put children's needs first, remain aware of their own needs, and meet them to the extent they can. Jane Lazarre's book, *The Mother Knot,* published in 1976 by McGraw-Hill and reprinted in 1997 by Duke University Press Books, speaks to this very well. As a MOSAC, mothers experience "double jeopardy:" the legal and child welfare systems assume mothers must have known, colluded with or contributed to the abuse. While in a few instances, this may be true, in the vast majority, it is not so, and mothers are unfairly blamed when they are **not** responsible for their child having been abused and, after learning about the abuse, sought to do all they could to protect their children. Mothers are frequently put in a defensive position at a time when they are desperately struggling to help their children, while dealing effectively with their own painful emotions. Due to the stressors faced by mothers in these circumstances, it is not surprising that so many develop PTSD and physical illnesses. It is a tribute to human resilience that so many mothers and their children recover from child sexual abuse traumas.

27. Plummer, C.A. (2006). The discovery process: What mothers see and do in gaining awareness of the sexual abuse of their children. *Child Abuse & Neglect, 30*(11), 1227–1237.

28. Block, S.D. & Williams, L.M. (2019). The prosecution of child sexual abuse: A partnership to improve outcomes. Office of Justice Programs' National Criminal Justice Reference Service. Document Number 252768 (March).

29. Clarke, M. (2019). Long-term recidivism studies show high arrest rates. *Prison Legal News: A Project of the Human Rights Defense Center, 30*(5), 60.

Chapter 6

30. Perry & Szalavitz, *op. cit.* (see Note 20 above).

31. Bolen, R.M. (2002). Guardian support of sexually abused children: A definition in search of a construct. *Trauma, Violence & Abuse, 3*(1), 40–67; Lovett, B.B. (2004). Child sexual abuse disclosure: Maternal response and other variables impacting the victim. *Child and Adolescent Social Work Journal, 21*(4), 355–371; Womack, M.E., Miller, G., & Lassiter, P. (1999). Helping mothers in incestuous families: An empathic approach. *Women & Therapy, 22*(4), 17–34.

32. Azzopardi, C., Alaggia, R., & Fallon, B. (2018). From Freud to feminism: Gendered constructions of blame across theories of child sexual abuse. *Journal of Child Sexual Abuse*, 27(4), 254–275; Cromer, L.D., & Goldsmith, R.E. (2010). Child sexual abuse myths: Attitudes, beliefs, and individual differences. *Journal of Child Sexual Abuse*, 19(6), 618–647; Toews, K., Cummings, J.A., & Zagrodney, J.L. (2016). Mother blame and the just world theory of child sexual abuse cases. *Journal of Interpersonal Violence*, 34(21–22), 4661-4686; Zagrodney, J.L., & Cummings, J.A. (2017). Qualitatively understanding mother fault after childhood sexual abuse. *Journal of Interpersonal Violence*, 7(1), https://doi.org/10.1177/0886260517723140

33. Fuller, G. (2016). Non-offending parents as secondary victims of child sexual assault. *Trends and Issues in Crime and Criminal Justice*, No.500; Kim, K., Noll, J.G., Putnam, F.W., & Trickett, P.K. (2007). Psychosocial characteristics of nonoffending mothers of sexually abused girls: Findings from a prospective, multigenerational study. *Child Maltreatment, 12*(4), 338–351.

34. McGuffey, C.S. (2005). Engendering trauma: Race, class, and gender reaffirmation after child sexual abuse. *Gender & Society, 19*(5), 621–643; Deblinger, E., Hathaway, C.R., Lippmann, J., & Steer, R. (1993). Psychosocial characteristics and correlates of symptom distress in nonoffending mothers of sexually abused children. *Journal of Interpersonal Violence*, 8(2), 155–168; Lafleur, C.T. (2009). Mothers' reactions to disclosure of sibling sexual abuse (Doctoral dissertation). Available from Dissertations and Theses database. (UMI No. 3358794); Triarhos-Suchlicki, S. (2008). Psychological functioning of nonoffending caregivers: The roles of attachment, parenting competence, child psychological functioning, and goodness-of-fit (Doctoral dissertation). Available from Dissertations and Theses database. (UMI No. 3285375); Womack et al., *op. cit.* (see Note 31 above).

35. Jülich, S.J. et al. Does grooming facilitate the development of Stockholm syndrome? The social work practice implications, *Aotearoa New Zealand Social Work* (2016). DOI: 10.11157/anzswj-vol28iss3id247

36. Kelley, S.J. (1986) Learned helplessness in the sexually abused child. *Issues in Comprehensive Pediatric Nursing, 9*(3), 193–207, DOI: 10.3109/01460868609029855 published online July 10, 2009.

Chapter 8

37. A study of "Stress Effects on Physical Health of Mothers of Sexually Abused Children," found that 90% of mothers studied had Acute Stress Disorder and dissociation; 87.9% met PTSD criteria and 43.8% scored high on somatic (physical) symptoms. Mothers whose children had disclosed 10 or more years ago were in the study group. Langston, M.E. (2011). Stress Effects on Physical Health of Mothers of Sexually Abused Children. Dissertation submitted to Northcentral University Graduate Faculty of the School of Behavioral and Health Sciences (September). My research was motivated by my own experience of severe illness and hospitalization in the aftermath of child sexual abuse disclosure and the impact of stress in my child's life and mine.

38. Langston, M. E. (2011). Stress Effects on Physical Health of Mothers of Sexually Abused Children. Dissertation Oral Defense, September 30. Dissertation submitted to Northcentral University Graduate Faculty of the School of Behavioral and Health Sciences (September).

APPENDIX

Selected Resources

This section provides selected resources including
- Hotlines;
- States and Territories Child Abuse and Child Sexual Abuse Reporting Toll-free Numbers and Websites;
- Information, Support and Resources;
- Prevention Information;
- Legal Advocacy;
- Resources for Youth with Sexual Behavior Problems;
- Selected Books;
- Selected Films, Videos and DVDs.

Hotlines for Help in Reporting Child Abuse and Child Sexual Abuse

Several Hotline numbers are listed below. Many are staffed 24/7. See also **Chapter 4** and www.mosac.net for reporting, investigation and assessment.

ChildHelp USA—National Child Abuse Hotline
www.childhelpusa.org

Hotline: 800.4.A.CHILD (800.422.4453)
Hotline staffed 24/7; professional counselors assist parents, child abuse victims, and individuals seeking information.
National Headquarters: 15757 N. 78th Street, Scottsdale, AZ 85260
Office: 480-922-8212; Fax: 480-922-7061

CyberTipline
http://www.cybertipline.com/
Toll-free line to report sexual exploitation of children on the web or other child pornography. Call **1-800-LOST** to report sexually exploited, abused, or missing children.

Darkness to Light
www.d2l.org
Phone: 866.FOR.LIGHT (866.367.5444) or text LIGHT to 741741
Email: darkness2light_2000@yahoo.com
Trained counselors available 24/7 with information on prevention, and response to child sexual abuse. National media campaign, advocacy and prevention training, national helpline, and work to change laws and policies to better protect children.

National Organization for Victim Assistance (NOVA)
www.trynova.org
Hotline: 800-TRY-NOVA (800-879-6682)
Email: nova@try-nova.org
Phone: 202-232-6682
Network of practitioners, organizations, and survivors committed to victim rights and services.

Rape, Abuse, and Incest National Network (RAINN)
www.rainn.org
Hotline: 1-800-656-HOPE (1-800-656-4673)
Hotline 24/7. RAINN partners with nearly 900 rape crisis centers across the country. Callers are automatically connected to local center for immediate help, information, referrals, or emotional support.
Email: rainnmail@aol.com

Stop It Now!
www.stopitnow.org or www.helpline@stopitnow.org
Website and Helpline offer support, information, and resources as a network of community-based programs.
Email: helpline@stopitnow.org
Office: 413-587-3500

U.S. States and Territories Child Abuse and Child Sexual Abuse Reporting Toll-Free Numbers and Websites

Alabama
https://dhr.alabama.gov/child-protective-services/child-abuse
-neglect-reporting/

Alaska
Toll-Free: (800) 478-4444
Email: HSS.DBH@Alaska.gov
http://dhss.alaska.gov/ocs/Pages/default.aspx
To report via email: ReportChildAbuse@alaska.gov

Arizona
Toll-Free: (888) SOS-CHILD (888-767-2445)
https://dcs.az.gov/
Arizona's Online Reporting Service for Mandated Reporters via secure website in non-emergency cases: https://dcs.az.gov/report-child-abuse

Arkansas
Toll-Free: (800) 482-5964
https://humanservices.arkansas.gov/

California
https://www.cdss.ca.gov/reporting/report-abuse/child-protective
-services/report-child-abuse

Colorado
Phone: (303) 866-5700
Phone: 1-844-264-5437
https://www.colorado.gov/cdhs

Connecticut
Toll-Free: (800) 842-2288
TDD: (800) 624-5518
https://portal.ct.gov/DCF

Delaware
Toll-Free: (800) 292-9582
https://kids.delaware.gov/

District of Columbia
Local (toll): (202) 671-SAFE (202-671-7233)
https://cfsa.dc.gov/service/report-child-abuse-and-neglect

Florida
Toll-Free: (800) 96-ABUSE (800-962-2873)
https://www.myflfamilies.com/service-programs/abuse-hotline/
Online Reporting http://www.myflfamilies.com/service-programs/
abuse-hotline

Georgia
Phone: (404) 657-3433
https://dfcs.georgia.gov/services/child-abuse-neglect

Guam
Phone: (671) 475-2653
Phone: (671) 475-2672

Hawaii
Local (toll): (808) 832-5300
http://humanservices.hawaii.gov/ssd/home/child-welfare-services/

Idaho
Phone: (208) 334-5437
Toll-Free: (800) 926-2588
https://healthandwelfare.idaho.gov/Children/AbuseNeglect/
ChildProtectionContactPhoneNumbers/tabid/475/Default.aspx

Illinois
Toll-Free: (800) 252-2873
Local (toll): (217) 524-2606
https://www2.illinois.gov/dcfs/safekids/reporting/Pages/index.aspx

Indiana
Toll-Free: (800) 800-5556
https://www.in.gov/dcs/

Iowa
Toll-Free: (800) 362-2178
https://dhs.iowa.gov/home

Kansas
Toll-Free: (800) 922-5330
http://www.dcf.ks.gov/Pages/Report-Abuse-or-Neglect.aspx
Online reporting for mandated reporters in non-emergency situations
http://www.dcf.ks.gov/services/PPS/Pages/KIPS/KIPSWebIntake.aspx

Kentucky
Toll-Free: (877) 597-2331
https://prd.webapps.chfs.ky.gov/reportabuse/home.aspx

Louisiana
Toll-Free: (855) 452-5437
http://dss.louisiana.gov/page/109
Online reporting portal for mandated reporters in non-emergency
situations https://mr.dcfs.la.gov/c/MR_PortalApp.app

Maine
Toll-Free: (800) 452-1999
TTY: (800) 963-9490
https://www.maine.gov/dhhs/ocfs/hotlines.htm

Maryland
http://dhr.maryland.gov/child-protective-services/reporting
-suspected-child-abuse-or-neglect/local-offices/

Massachusetts
Toll-Free: (800) 792-5200
https://www.mass.gov/child-abuse-and-neglect

Michigan
Toll-Free: (855) 444-3911
Fax: (616) 977-1154
https://www.michigan.gov/mdhhs/0,5885,7-339-73971_7119---,00
.html

Minnesota
https://mn.gov/dhs/report-abuse/

Mississippi
Phone: (601) 432-4570
Toll-Free: (800) 222-8000
https://www.mdcps.ms.gov/report-child-abuse-neglect/
https://reportabuse.mdcps.ms.gov/
Reporting via online system or by downloading the MDCPS Report
Child Abuse mobile app https://www.mdcps.ms.gov/report-child
-abuse-neglect/

Missouri
Toll-Free: (800) 392-3738
https://dss.mo.gov/cd/keeping-kids-safe/can.htm

Montana
Toll-Free: (866) 820-5437
https://dphhs.mt.gov/cfsd/index

Nebraska
Phone: (402) 471-3121
Toll-Free: (800) 652-1999
http://dhhs.ne.gov/Pages/Child-Abuse.aspx

Nevada
http://dcfs.nv.gov/Programs/CWS/CPS/CPS/

New Hampshire
Phone: (603) 271-6562
Toll-Free: (800) 894-5533
https://www.dhhs.nh.gov/dcyf/cps/stop.htm

New Jersey
Toll-Free: (877) 652-2873
TDD: (800) 835-5510
TTY: (800) 835-5510
https://www.nj.gov/dcf/reporting/hotline/

New Mexico
Toll-Free: (855) 333-7233
https://cyfd.org/

New York
Toll-Free: (800) 342-3720
TDD: (800) 369-2437
Local (toll): (518) 474-8740
https://ocfs.ny.gov/main/cps/Default.asp

North Carolina
https://www.ncdhhs.gov/

North Dakota
http://www.nd.gov/dhs/services/childfamily/cps/#reporting

Ohio
Toll-Free: (855) 642-4453
http://jfs.ohio.gov/ocf/reportchildabuseandneglect.stm

Oklahoma
Toll-Free: (800) 522-3511
https://www.ok.gov/health/Family_Health/Family_Support_and
_Prevention_Service/Oklahoma_Child_Abuse_Hotline/index.html

Oregon
Toll-Free: (855) 503-SAFE (7233)
https://www.oregon.gov/dhs/children/child-abuse/Pages/
Reporting-Numbers.aspx

Pennsylvania
Toll-Free: (800) 932-0313
TDD: (866) 872-1677
https://www.dhs.pa.gov/contact/Pages/Report-Abuse.aspx

Puerto Rico
Toll-Free: (800) 981-8333
Local (toll): (787) 749-1333

Rhode Island
Phone: (401) 528-3500
Toll-Free: (800) RI-CHILD (800-742-4453)
http://www.dcyf.ri.gov/child-protective-services/

South Carolina
Local (toll): (803) 898-7318
https://dss.sc.gov/abuseneglect/report-child-abuse-and-neglect/

South Dakota
TTY: (877) 244-0864
https://dss.sd.gov/childprotection/

Tennessee
Toll-Free: (877) 237-0004
https://www.tn.gov/dcs/program-areas/child-safety/reporting/
child-abuse.html

Texas
Toll-Free: (800) 252-5400
https://www.dfps.state.tx.us/Contact_Us/report_abuse.asp

U.S. Virgin Islands
http://www.dhs.gov.vi/contact/index.html

Utah
Phone: 1-855-323-3237
https://dcfs.utah.gov/

Vermont
After hours: (800) 649-5285
https://dcf.vermont.gov/protection/reporting

Virginia
Toll-Free: (800) 552-7096
Local (toll): (804) 786-8536
https://www.dss.virginia.gov/family/cps/index.cgi

Washington
Toll-Free: (800) 562-5624
Toll-Free: (866) END-HARM (866-363-4276)
TTY: (800) 624-6186
https://www.dcyf.wa.gov/safety/report-abuse

West Virginia
Toll-Free: (800) 352-6513
https://dhhr.wv.gov/bcf/Services/Pages/Centralized-Intake-for
-Abuse-and-Neglect.aspx

Wisconsin
https://dcf.wisconsin.gov/reportabuse

Wyoming
https://www.wyomingcac.org/prevent-child-abuse/reporting
-child-abuse

Information, Support, and Resources

Bikers Against Child Abuse International
www.bacaworld.org
Biker organization emotionally and physically supports abused
children. Raises funds for prevention; speaks out against child abuse.

Child Welfare Information Gateway
https://www.childwelfare.gov/topics/can/
Child abuse information and resources.

Male Survivor
www.malesurvivor.org
Research, education, advocacy, and activism for sexual abuse
prevention and treatment. Retreats, conferences, and chat rooms.

Mama Bear Effect
www.themamabeareffect.org
Educational resources for sexual abuse awareness and protection of
children.

MeTooMovement
www.metoomvmt.org
Built on the #metoo movement founded in 2006 by Tarana Burke, the
website offers information for women (and men) of all ages on sexual
violence, including healing, action, intersectionality, learning more,
glossary, resources, current issues and initiatives.

The National Children's Advocacy Center (NCAC)
www.nationalcac.org
https://www.nationalcac.org/find-a-cac/
Office: 256-533-KIDS
The first Children's Advocacy Center in the U.S. Non-profit providing
prevention, intervention, and treatment services to abused children
and their families.

Pandora's Project
www.pandys.org
Support for victims; message board, chat room, free lending library,
and resources.

Parents United
www.parents-united.net
Treatment for child sexual abuse; links include state chapter information.

Psychology Today
https://www.psychologytoday.com/us/groups/sexual-abuse/
Lists of support groups by state.

Stop Abuse Campaign
www.stopabusecampaign.org
Education and resources on child sexual abuse and prevention.

Stop the Silence: Stop Child Abuse, Inc.
www.stopcsa.org
Helpline: 1-888-PREVENT
Email: helpline@stopitnow.org
Phone: 1-866-397-2309
Support, information, and resources for keeping children safe.

Survivors of Incest Anonymous (SIA)
www.siawso.org
World service office assisting local SIA support groups and individuals. Publishes and sells incest survivor literature, maintains meeting directory.
Office: 410-893-3322

Survivors Network of those Abused by Priests (SNAP)
www.snapnetwork.org
Self-help adult survivors' organization supporting healing, justice and institutional change. Local chapters and support groups. Peer counseling, support group contact information, online discussion, library resources.

Prevention Information

Avoiding Sexual Dangers
www.avoidingsexualdangers.net
Information, resources, links for parents to protect their children. Parent checklists, controls, how-to videos, and blog.

Child Abuse Watch
www.abusewatch.net
Child abuse prevention network, easy-to-access and understand child abuse prevention information.

Child Help Speak Up Be Safe Prevention Education Curriculum
www.childhelp.org/subs/childhelp-speak-up-be-safe/
Helps children and teen learn skills to prevent or interrupt cycles of neglect, bullying and child abuse—physical, emotional, and sexual.

Child Lures Prevention
www.childluresprevention.com
Child, family, and community education to prevent child sexual abuse. Resources on sexual exploitation, abduction, internet crime, predators' lures and avoidance skills.

Child Molestation Research & Prevention Institute
www.childmolestationprevention.org
National science-based nonprofit organization to prevent child sexual abuse through research, education, and family support.

International Center for Assault Prevention
www.internationalcap.org
Prevention of interpersonal violence through research, education, and training. Child Assault Prevention Project (CAP).

KidSafe Foundation
www.kidsafefoundation.org
Prevention information for parents, children, and educators.

Mothers Against Sexual Predators At Large (MASPAL)
http://maspal.org
Protect children from sexual predators with information and support for victims and their families.

National Center for Missing and Exploited Children (NCMEC)
www.ncmec.org
National clearinghouse for information on missing children and prevention of child victimization.

Prevent Child Abuse America (PCAA)
www.preventchildabuse.org
Office: 312-663-3520
National volunteer-based organization for child abuse prevention through research, education, and advocacy.

Legal Advocacy

Crew Janci LLP
www.crewjanci.com
Nationally recognized law firm providing free consultations for civil child abuse cases.

Court Appointed Special Advocates for Children (CASA)
www.casaforchildren.org
Judicially appointed community volunteers who advocate for safety and well-building of children removed from their homes due to parental abuse or neglect.

National Association for Counsel of Children (NACC)
www.naccchildlaw.org
Email: advocate@NACCchildlaw.org
Phone: 888-828-6222
Non-profit professional membership organization dedicated to legal system quality child representation and protection. Referrals and at-cost educational materials on children and the law.

National Center for Victims of Crime (NCVC)
www.victimsofcrime.org
Office: 800-394-2255
Support, information, and referral for crime victims. Helpline, crisis intervention, advocacy, criminal procedure assistance; local attorneys and counseling services referrals.

National Criminal Justice Reference Service (NCJRS)
www.ncjrs.gov
One of the world's most extensive publicly available criminal and juvenile information and services sources.

National Organization for Victim Assistance (NOVA)
www.trynova.org
Email: nova@try-nova.org
Phone: 202-232-6682
Network of practitioners, organizations, and survivors committed to victim rights and services.

Resources for Youth with Sexual Behavior Problems

National Adolescent Perpetration Network (NAPN)
www.kempe.org
Email: questions@kempe.org
Office: 303-864-5192
Cooperative professional network serving sexually abusive youth, providing treatment information and referrals.

National Center on Sexual Behavior of Youth
www.ncsby.org
Information about sexual development and youth sexual behavior problems.

Books

Books are valuable healing tools. Learning, reading and *identifying* with other mothers' stories helps you understand your feelings and situation. Reading about children's recovery experiences helps you better understand your child and his, her, or their feelings.

For MOTHERS

Adams, Caren & Fay, Jennifer. (1992) *Helping your child recover from sexual abuse.* University of Washington Press. Practical guidance to help your child cope, recover, and feel safe again.

Bass, Ellen & Davis, Laura. (2008). The courage to heal (4th Ed.). HarperCollins. Twentieth anniversary edition of classic guide for women survivors of child sexual abuse.

Brohl, Kathryn with Potter, Joyce. (2004). *When your child has been molested: A parent's guide to healing and recovery.* (Revised Ed.) Jossey-Bass. Guide for parents; abuse, disclosure, reporting, and recovery.

Burke Harris, Nadine. (2018). *The deepest well: Healing the long-term effects of childhood adversity.* Houghton Mifflin Harcourt. Must-read by a pediatrician child trauma specialist, now California Surgeon General, about long-term effects of child abuse.

Chesler, Phyllis (2011). *Mothers on trial: The battle for children and custody.* Lawrence Hill. Describes key issues for mothers in custody conflicts.

Daugherty, Lynn. (2013). *Listening and talking to your sexually abused child.* CreateSpace. A brief beginner's guide for parents of sexually abused children.

Davis, Laura. (2002). *I thought we'd never speak again.* HarperCollins. Gripping, first-person accounts of reconciling relationships damaged by betrayal, anger, and misunderstanding, including abuse.

Davis, Laura. (1990). *The courage to heal workbook for women and men survivors of child sexual abuse.* Harper & Row. Useful self-understanding and healing exercises.

de Becker, Gavin. (1999). *Protecting the gift: Keeping children and teenagers safe.* Dial Press. Safety skills, warning sexual abuse signs, parent safety strategies for children and teens.

Ensler, Eve (2019). *The Apology.* Bloomsbury Press. A powerful, moving and compelling imagined apology by the abusive father of a renowned playwright.

Freyd, Jennifer and Birrell, P. (2013). *Blind to betrayal: Why we fool ourselves we aren't being fooled.* Wiley. Personal accounts about betrayal, broken trust, abuse and effects of dissociation.

Gray, Lisa R. (2017). *They don't tell: Child abuse: A mother's perspective.* CreateSpace. Powerful account of a mother's experience of her daughter's abuse and recovery.

Harrison, Kayla and Kaplan, Cynthia S., et al. (2018) *Fighting back: what an Olympic champion's story can teach us about recognizing and preventing child abuse.* Guilford Press. Keeping kids safe, grooming signs, why kids stay silent, helping children recover.

Johnson, Toni Cavanaugh. (2015) *Understanding children's sexual behaviors: What's normal and healthy.* NEARI Press. Healthy sexual behavior and development in children to age twelve; abusive sexual behavior by children.

Levine, Peter A. (2008). *Healing Trauma: A Pioneering Program for Restoring the Wisdom of Your Body.* SoundsTrue. Describes Somatic Experiencing approach to healing from trauma.

Levine, Peter A. & Kline, Maggie. (2008). *Trauma-proofing your kids: A parents' guide for instilling confidence, joy, and resilience.* (2008). North Atlantic Books. Child trauma; teaching resilience, confidence, and joy.

Levy, Barrie, & Giggans, Patricia. (1999). *What parents need to know about dating violence.* Seal Press (Hachette). Information, advice, and stories from parents and teens; teaching teens self-protection and building healthy relationships.

Levy-Peck, Jennifer Y. *Healing the harm done: A parents' guide to helping your child overcome the effects of sexual abuse.* (2009). Hope Through Healing Publications. Your child's emotions and behaviors; your reactions.

Merryn, Erin. (2009). *Living for today: A memoir. From incest and molestation to fearlessness and forgiveness.* Health Communications. Personal story of recovery from childhood sexual abuse and activism for change.

Morris, Rick. (2006). *Protecting and parenting sexually abused children: Tools for parents and caregivers.* Lulu.com.

Ostis, Connie M. (2002). *What's happening in our family?* Safer Society Press. Uses metaphors and simple language to explain sexual abuse and its effects on families.

Perry, Bruce D. & Szalavit, M. (2017). *The boy who was raised as a dog and other stories from a child psychiatrist's notebook: What traumatized children can teach us about loss, love, and healing.* Basic Books. Ten case studies by leading child trauma psychiatrist about trauma, reducing negative outcomes and helping children heal.

Sax, Robin. *Predators and child molesters: What every parent needs to keep kids safe.* (2009). Prometheus Books. A must-read for all parents seeking to protect their children.

Sichel, Mark. (2004). *Healing from family rifts: Ten steps to finding peace after being cut off from a family member.* McGraw-Hill. A moving, practical book with useful tools for addressing and healing family rifts.

Silva, Claire. *A child's heart speaks: Surviving sexual abuse.* (2006). AuthorHouse. True story of two children who survived older half-brother's sexual abuse, victims' struggles and relationship with the perpetrator.

Tobin, Pnina & Kessner, Sue. (2002). *Keeping kids safe: A child sexual abuse prevention manual* (2nd ed.). Nashville, TN: Hunter House. Helps teach children safety skills and prevention strategies.

van der Kolk, Bessel. (2014). *The Body Keeps The Score: Brain, Mind, and Body in the Healing of Trauma.* Penguin Books. Describes how trauma changes body and brain and offers innovative paths to recovery.

Wiklund, Patricia. (1995) *Sleeping with a stranger: How I survived marriage to a child molester.* Adams Media Corp. Story of psychologist whose husband sexually abused their child. Emotional responses, actions, myth shattering, and accurate information about mothers' and children's recovery.

Wurtele, Sandy & Berkower, Feather. *Off limits: A parents' guide to keeping kids safe from sexual abuse.* (2010). Safer Society Press. How parents can keep their children safe from sex offenders.

For CHILDREN

Akers, Ellery. (2009). *Sarah's waterfall: A healing story about sexual abuse.* Safer Society Press. First year of recovery from sexual abuse. Ages 7–14.

Berenzweig, Sallie, Benjoseph, Cherie, & Cohen, Lilah. (2017). *My body is special and belongs to me!* KidSafe Foundation. Teaching personal safety. Grades Preschool–3.

Connor, Teresa. (2010). *Good touch bad touch: Learning about proper and improper touches.* CreateSpace. Helps parents teach good and bad touches. Ages 3–10.

Deaton, Wendy & Johnson, Kendall. *No More Hurt: A child's workbook about recovering from abuse.* (2002). Hunter House. Creative, child-friendly workbook; exercises for healing and growth. Ages 6–12.

Edelman, Robert D. (2013). *My private parts are private!* CreateSpace. Teaching safe touching. Grades 3–7.

Fitzgerald, Pattie. (2011). *No trespassing—This is my body!* Safely Ever After Media. Helps parents reduce risks and keep children safe from predators. Ages 4–8.

Foltz, Linda Lee. (2003). *Kids helping kids break the silence of sexual abuse.* Lighthouse Point Press. Kids share true survival stories. Child–Teen.

Geisler, Dagmar. (2018). *I won't go with strangers.* Sky Pony. Helps parents explain dangers of going with strangers. Ages 3–6.

Geisler, Dagmar. (2014). *My body belongs to me from my head to my toes.* Sky Pony. Difference between appropriate and inappropriate touch. Ages 3–6.

Jenson, Kristen. (2017). *Good pictures bad pictures Jr.* Glen Cove Press. Helps parents protect children from internet dangers. Ages 3–9.

Jenson, Kristen & Poyner, Gail. (2016). *Good touch bad touch: porn-proofing today's young kids.* Glen Cove Press. Dangers of pornography and how to reject it. Grades 1–8.

Jessie. *(1991). Please tell! A child's story about sexual abuse.* Hazelden. Written and illustrated by a girl sexually molested by a family member, telling other children to "tell." Grades Preschool–2.

King, Kimberly (2016). *I said no! A kid-to-kid guide to keeping private parts private* (3rd Ed.). Boulden. Helps kids set healthy boundaries for their private parts. Ages 5–11.

Krebs, Lindsay K. and Merritt, Kimberly (2020). *It's not your fault.* Independently published. A sexually abused girl tells her story in a child-friendly way. Includes tips and guidelines for parents and caregivers to read with their child age 5–10 who has been sexually abused.

Malver, Anne (2019). *My safe place: A mindful journey toward healing and well-being.* Anne Malver. Takes child on a journey into their own mind to find a place of emotional safety and comfort. Grades 1–5.

Malver, Anne. (2019). *My yucky feeling: Preventing child sexual abuse.* Anne Malver. Teaches children to trust their "gut" if something doesn't feel right. Grades 1–5.

Marnach, Kayla J.W. (2018). *My body's mine: A book on body boundaries and sexual abuse prevention.* CreateSpace. Body boundaries and sexual abuse prevention. K–5.

Merryn, Erin (2005). *Stolen innocence: Triumphing over a childhood broken by abuse.* HCI. Memoir based on personal diary during abuse written by originator of Erin's Law, advocate, and creator of curriculum used throughout the U.S.

Moore-Mallinos, Jennifer (2005). *Do you have a secret? Let's talk about it.* BES. Teaches children how to talk about their secrets. Grades Preschool–2.

Sanders, Jayneen. (2017). *Let's talk about body boundaries, consent, & respect: Teach children about body ownership, respect, feelings, choices and recognizing bullying behaviors.* Educate to Empower. Teaches children about boundaries, feelings and choices. K–4.

Sanders, Jayneen, (2015). *No means no! Teaching children about personal boundaries, respect and consent; empowering kids by respecting their choices and their right way to say, "no."* Educate to Empower. Teaches voice, rights, and boundaries. K–3.

Simeone, Adrianne (2018). *My body is special and private.* Mama Bear Effect. Introduces privacy and body safety. Age 2 up.

Spelman, Cornelia (1997). *Your body belongs to you.* Albert Whitman & Company. Teaches children how to say "no" to hugs, kisses, and touching. Preschool–3.

Strauss, Susan Farber (2013). *Healing days: A guide for kids who have experienced trauma.* APA Magination. Teaching children about trauma, recovery and coping skills. Ages 8–12.

For ADOLESCENTS

Bean, Barbara & Bennett, Shari (1997). *The me nobody knows: A guide for teen survivors.* Jossey-Bass. Sexual abuse and recovery workbook for adolescents. Ages 12–21.

Byers, Ann (2016). *Sexual assault and abuse: Confronting violence against women.* Rosen. Teen awareness about sexual abuse. Grades 7–12.

Daugherty, Lynn (2007). *Why me? Help for victims of child sexual abuse (Even if they are adults now)* (4th Ed.). Cleanan. Help for all ages on sexual abuse and recovery.

Feuereisen, Patti (2018). *Invisible girls: The truth about sexual abuse: A book for teen girls, young women, and everyone who cares about them.* (3rd Ed.) Seal. Preventing, reporting, and recovering from sexual abuse. Grades 9 & up.

Finney, Lynne D. (1992). *Reach for the Rainbow: Advanced healing for survivors of sexual abuse.* Tarcher-Perigee. Positive, compassionate healing advice for survivors. Teen-Young Adult.

Lehman, Carolyn (2005). *Strong at the heart: How it feels to heal from sexual abuse.* Farrar, Strauss and Giroux. Survivors discuss abuse, healing, and moving forward. Grades 9–12.

Lohmann, Raychelle & Raja, Sheela (2016). *The sexual trauma workbook for teen girls: A guide to recovery from sexual assault & abuse.* New Harbinger. Hope, inspiration, and recovery guidance. Ages 13–17.

Mather, Cynthia (2014). *How long does it hurt? A guide to recovering from incest and sexual abuse for teenagers, their friends, and their families.* Jossey Bass. Recovery from incest and sexual abuse.

Pledge, Deanna S. (2002). *When something feels wrong: A survival guide about abuse for young people.* Free Spirit. Dealing with abuse positively. Grades 8–12.

Selected FILMS, VIDEOS, and DVDs

Note: Viewing films may add to your understanding of sexual abuse; they also may be upsetting, as content may trigger reactions in you or others. View privately prior to inviting a family member to join.

Eastwood, Clint (Director). (2003). *Mystic River.* Warner Brothers. Amazon and Netflix. Academy Award winning film based on novel about a man who experienced sexual abuse as a boy.

Fox, Jennifer (Director). (2018). *The tale.* United States: Gamechanger Films. HBO, Netflix and HBO. True story about grooming and sexual abuse in equestrian coaching and competition.

Hackford, Taylor (Director). (1995). *Delores Claiborne.* Castle Rock Entertainment; Columbia Pictures. Amazon and Netflix. Based on a Stephen King novel about a woman married to an abusive, alcoholic man; she discovers his molestation of her daughter, and murders him.

Hallstrom, Lasse (Director). (1999). *Cider House Rules.* Miramax Films; Film Colony. Amazon and Netflix. Based on John Irving's book; he was a victim of child sexual abuse. A man leaves the orphanage where he was raised, saw and experienced abuse.

Johnson, Lamont (Director) (1990). *Voices within: The lives of Truddi Chase*. Australian Broadcasting. YouTube. Based on Truddi Chase's autobiography, *When rabbit howls*, about her therapy for childhood sexual abuse beginning at age two, which resulted in Multiple Personality Disorder.

Kramer, Lloyd (Director). (2000). *The Mary Kay Letourneau story: All American girl*. Grosso-Jacobson Productions. YouTube, Amazon, and Netflix. Based on Mary Kay Letourneau's sexual abuse of her sixth-grade student, having his child, and social and legal consequences of the crime.

Levinson, Barry (Director). (1996). *Sleepers*. Warner Brothers. Amazon, Google Play, Netflix. Oscar-winning film, reported to be a true account of four boys sent to a reform school where they were physically and sexually abused.

McCarthy, Tom (Director). (2015). *Spotlight*. Open Road. Amazon and Netflix. A major motion picture about the exposure of child sexual abuse in the Catholic Church in Boston.

Moorhouse, Jocelyn (Director). (1997). *A Thousand Acres*. Walt Disney; Mill Creek. Amazon and Netflix. Based on Jane Smiley's Pulitzer prize-winning novel about daughters sexually abused by their father as children who kept the secret from one another until adulthood.

Rapkin, Brett (Director). (2019). *The weight of gold*. United States: HBO. Amazon and HBO. Documentary about sexual abuse in competitive gymnastics, the perpetrator's trial, victims' statements and the judge's remarks.

Reed, Dan (Director). (2019). *Leaving Neverland*. HBO. Amazon, HBO and Netflix. Prize-winning documentary about Michael Jackson's alleged grooming of parents and children. HBO showing was followed by HBO/OWN Oprah Winfrey Special with mothers, victims and survivors.

Streisand, Barbra (Director). (1991). *The prince of tides.* Sony Pictures. Amazon and Netflix. Story of a man's therapy and exploration of his childhood, including severe trauma, sexual assault, and domestic violence.

Washington, Denzel (Director). (2002). *Antwone Fisher.* Fox Searchlight. Amazon and Netflix. An inspiring story of an angry young man's healing, based on Antwone Fisher's memoir, *Finding Fish*, on his recovery from physical, emotional, and sexual abuse.

Zlotoff, Lee David (Director). (1996). *The Spitfire Grill.* Columbia; Castle Rock. Amazon, Google Play, Netflix, YouTube. Based on the story of a young woman struggling to fit into a new community after release from prison for killing her sexually abusive stepfather.

YOUTUBE and other Online VIDEOS About Sexual Abuse

Dozens of YouTube videos of moving personal stories and excellent information on sexual abuse are available online. Exploration of these can increase your understanding of both your child and yourself, with help in healing and recovery. Some organizations listed above also offer online videos.

Janeen Bradley's *Safety Kids* songs for children are favorites, teaching safety skills to engaging music. The Yell and Run song: https://youtu.be/ Pf3nyYShlpg; all the original Safety Kids songs: https://www.amazon .com/Safety-Kids-Vol-Personal/dp/B07NKK9VZD/ref=nodl_

NOTES

Made in United States
Troutdale, OR
09/11/2024

22740773R00116